HARM TO HEALING

Felicia Carbajal

HARM TO HEALING

A Pathway to Abolition

The Carceral Studies Collection

Collection Editor

Ian Cummins & Louis Mendoza

LPp

First published in 2025 by Lived Places Publishing

British Library Cataloguing in Publication Data
A CIP record for this book is available from the British Library

ISBN: 9781916704589 (pbk)
ISBN: 9781916704602 (ePDF)
ISBN: 9781916704596 (ePUB)

The right of Felicia Carbajal to be identified as the Author of this work has been asserted by them in accordance with the Copyright, Design and Patents Act 1988.

Cover design by Fiachra McCarthy
Book design by Rachel Trolove of Twin Trail Design
Typeset by Newgen Publishing UK

Lived Places Publishing
Long Island
New York 11789

www.livedplacespublishing.com

Abstract

Harm to Healing is a powerful memoir and exploration of systemic injustice written by Felicia Carbajal, a Queer, Latinx community organizer and survivor of the drug war and violent crime. The book opens with personal reflections on Carbajal's upbringing in California, where poverty and community resilience shaped their early understanding of justice, identity, and the importance of solidarity across diverse communities. This narrative is interwoven with a deep critique of systemic inequalities, emphasizing how policies like the War on Drugs and mass incarceration disproportionately impact marginalized groups, including BIPOC and LGBTQ+ individuals.

Throughout the book, Carbajal recounts their own experiences of incarceration, delving into the harsh realities of the prison system. They highlight the dehumanizing processes faced by incarcerated individuals, especially those from marginalized backgrounds, while also capturing moments of community-building within carceral spaces. Their reflections shed light on how the carceral system further entrenches social inequities, separating individuals from their communities and hope. The author's story serves as a testament to the resilience and agency of those who survive these oppressive structures, offering a raw, honest portrayal of the emotional and psychological toll of incarceration.

They also emphasize the role of storytelling and activism as tools for healing and community empowerment. They discuss their transition from being a survivor of harm to becoming an advocate for change, utilizing their lived experiences to support others impacted by criminalization. The book is both a personal journey and a call to action, advocating for a world where justice is rooted in compassion and collective liberation. Ultimately, *Harm to Healing* is an urgent appeal for transformative justice, inviting readers to reimagine a society free from the violence of incarceration, where healing and accountability replace punishment.

Keywords

Abolition

Incarceration

Mutual Aid

Reentry

Systemic Injustice

Trauma-Informed

Storytelling

Resilience

Transformative Justice

Criminalization

LGBTQ+ Advocacy

Intersectionality

Community Empowerment

Healing

Mass Incarceration

Contents

Introduction

I'm Felicia Carbajal, a Queer, Latinx, drug war and violent crime survivor, and a community organizer. My fondest childhood memories involved visiting my grandfather's home in the housing projects in Fresno, California. I loved Tata, his community's diversity, and cook-outs featuring international dishes made with pride, love, and, our common denominator, poverty. At Fresno, I learned the meaning of community, the importance of sharing, and how coming together over food could bridge cultural divides. There, I had friends of all races and nationalities who easily shared what little everyone had as a form of celebration. The first Saturday of the month was always a festive time as it was when most folks got their monthly social safety net checks.

I didn't realize I was poor. I didn't understand how our justice system was affecting people like me or that I would become a statistic, too. Growing up facing intergenerational poverty, broken social safety nets (which never felt safe), and institutions perpetuating violence and harm deepened my desire for equity and fairness. I immersed myself in intersectional struggles, including civil disobedience in the 1990s during the AIDS Crisis, California's marriage equality movement, cannabis legalization, and efforts to end the drug war.

Although there are many of us who, despite growing up in underserved communities, broke the generational cycles of poverty and never saw the insides of institutions, I was not that lucky. My path led me to being incarcerated, while this was far from the trajectory my childhood accomplishments would suggest. The same goes with being harmed and participating in harm—many of us don't necessarily see ourselves in these spaces, but through a series of challenges, we find ourselves there. Incarceration fundamentally separates people from the community—most importantly, the sense of safety in the community—and from hope. I am grateful I never lost hope even in my darkest moments. I knew we deserved to be free and that the harm done to us was wrong.

Today I am privileged to be serving as the Executive Director of the Social Impact Center (TSIC), a Los Angeles based hub for justice-impacted community members. After serving over six years in prison, I am grateful to share my insights and hope for us. This book examines the lived experience of survivors of harm and incarceration while diving into the heart of disinvestment and incarceration as to how our lack of safety is fundamentally linked to racial, gender, and sexual orientation, as well as other forms of inequality. The life I get to explore and question on a daily basis in the community reminds me that I am beyond blessed.

The experiences shared demonstrate how the language of abolition directly answers the lack of safety and insecurity that mass incarceration worsens and offers a way to envision a natural end to this carceral world. The world I dream of! The world I long for. The world my ancestors remind me that is possible. The world I hope you help give life to in community.

1
How It Began

Learning Objectives

1. Understand historical and personal narratives.
2. Examine how firsthand experiences with socioeconomic disparities during childhood influence perceptions of poverty, privilege, and social justice advocacy.
3. Reflect on educational influence.

As a bicentennial baby (1976) born into a Mexican American family whose ancestors have occupied the desert southwest for a millennium, I feel little to no connection to an anniversary year that celebrates all the harms that the founding of the United States has caused and continues to cause. While my birth was a time of celebration for my large Mexican American family (I have 72 first cousins), it was also when the seeds of justice and equality were planted in me. You see, my father was an underemployed factory and farm worker, and my mother was a newly found housewife who had experienced the harms of this world at a very young age, including the foster care system in the 1950s–1960s. I was born into the generational harms of the lasting effects of colonization and displacement of the Mexican people. The fight for healing and justice is rooted in the large, multigenerational, poverty-stricken family I hail from.

While I did not grow up in the housing projects myself, my mother did, and my fondest childhood memories exist in moments spent with my grandfather there. The "Projects" are government-built homes provided to low-income families as part of a social safety net—think giant apartment complexes that often times were neglected. They typically sit in a less desirable neighborhood or area of the town. You apply to be able to live there. This ecosystem, rife with government bureaucracy, was built around housing. While many jobs opened up for the community to support their function, little went into helping the community members uplift themselves from the situation in human-first approaches.

My grandfather had left Texas at a very early age, in his early teens, in search of a better life. He initially moved to Arizona, where he met my grandmother, but ultimately landed in the Central Valley of California. The area that I grew up in, Fresno, is commonly referred to as the breadbasket of the United States. California's agriculture industry is pivotal in the national and global food supply, as the Central Valley currently account for two-thirds of the fruits and nuts produced. I don't know those stats from the 1940s to the 1950s, but I imagine they were impressive. My grandparents, who were farm workers, traveled the state seeking opportunities to support their growing family.

At the heart of California's agricultural success are the migrant farm workers who perform the labor-intensive tasks essential to the industry. Despite their critical role, these workers often face harsh working conditions, low wages, and inadequate labor protections. Many live in poverty, with limited access to healthcare and education, highlighting significant social failings within the industry. Efforts to improve labor conditions, such as advocating for fair wages, better working environments, and more robust legal protections, are essential for the well-being of these workers as well as the sustainability and ethical integrity of California's agricultural sector. The problems of the past continue to remain the problems of today for many.

All I remember from my Tata is a deep sense of "community," which was necessary for our survival as a people. It was incumbent that we treated everyone we encountered with dignity and respect. While I didn't know I was poor until I was much older, I knew we were different. I knew I could visit my grandfather, fondly known as Tata (a now uncommon name previously used in Northern Mexico for grandpa), and enter a cornucopia of diversity where Mama, my Black grandmother who was raising her grandkids, shared a wall with my Tata and was a surrogate mother to my own mother, whose mom died when she was seven months old. This woman shared love with everyone who stepped into her home. She bought me my first doll, which I cherished deeply because it came from her. This woman shared so much passion through adversity with me and my family. Her grandson made the best ribs I have ever eaten, and today, I pride myself on remembering the mustard that Johnny had always taught me to add.

The first Saturday of the month (after government-issued welfare checks were sent out) was typically a community potluck day. Most if not all residents received government aid for the month, allowing them one celebratory—and often decadent—meal they all chose to share with their neighbors. I remember trying Soul, Vietnamese, Cambodian, Laotian, and Filipino food for the first time at one of the many monthly community cookouts

I could attend. The pride that these people had in their dishes was phenomenal. I fell in love with Lumpia (Filipino egg roll) on one of these Saturdays—I have yet to meet a Lumpia I can't appreciate.

Later, I learned that my Tata marched with Cesar Chavez from Delano to Sacramento in the United Farm Workers' early days. He was a regular face at meetings that addressed the harsh conditions people like him had experienced. He used his and his late wife's story to fight for better conditions for farm workers. The legacy I come from is that of folk who work and fight hard for equity and justice for people experiencing poverty and striving to fulfill America's promises to their families.

520 S. 11th

I was initially brought home to a small apartment two blocks away, and ultimately spent my elementary school years living less than a mile away from the projects.

"My name is Felicia Carbajal. I live at 520 S. 11th" was the beginning of a familiar story my mom would talk about the first time I got lost in a store and what she found me saying to a stranger. All of my experiences in this southeast area of the town propelled me forward. It is incredible what core memories are. I will never forget the address and telephone number of the house I grew up in. It was a duplex that sat at the corner of the block. It had two different addresses for the units and was a place united and filled with love and compassion always.

My journey toward becoming a politicized individual began early, shaped by profound experiences that challenged my understanding of justice, fairness, and identity. Growing up just a mile from the housing projects in the southeast area of my town, I was exposed to stark disparities in wealth and opportunities from a young age. One of my earliest memories that deeply impacted me was in first grade under the guidance of Mrs. Irene Hara—a teacher who had experienced the Japanese internment during World War II. Her poignant stories about the annual County Fair, held in stables that once housed Japanese Americans, opened my eyes to the injustices of history and sparked a sense of empathy and social consciousness within me.

Mrs. Hara's narrative not only introduced me to the dark corners of American history but also highlighted the resilience of marginalized communities. As a child, I couldn't fully grasp the magnitude of injustice faced by Mrs. Hara's family and others who endured the internment camps. Walking through those same stables where families were stripped of their humanity and housed like animals brought the reality of their suffering vividly to life in my young mind. This early exposure planted seeds of empathy and a burgeoning awareness of systemic inequalities that would continue to grow throughout my life.

I fondly remember Mrs. Hara continuing the trend of folks who influenced my life and understanding of the world. Little did I know that a trip to the annual county fair would awaken me at such an early age. Mrs. Hara, who had experienced Japanese internment in the United States, shared with us as first graders both the excitement of going to the annual county fair and the painful truth about the history of that place—it had housed Japanese Americans in the horse stables. And as a six-year-old, my mind was blown. I had no idea: not only that this was a part of our history but the fact, which Mrs. Hara shared, that my teacher's father, who was a dentist, and his whole family had to pack up their homes to go live in the stables as they waited to be shipped across the country. A dentist! An admirable profession and yet this is how he was treated—this struck me deeply indeed.

Mrs. Hara recollected that when they finally returned to the only home she had known in Fresno, it was in poor condition, and everything they had built with the business was gone. As a six-year-old traveling to that fair and walking through the stables to see animals, I cried because I envisioned myself being forced to live in horse stables with my family stripped of their entire dignity, and it shook me. It took a lot of comforting for this overly emotional child to calm down, including having my mom come and meet us so I could continue my fair experience.

And, of course, it was not lost on me that the government would build these social safety nets, "The Projects"—the housing projects on the next block—behind this very area that had brought so much shame to the city I grew up in. While many of us experience different poverty levels, I could recognize within my understanding that there were layers within these. I wasn't as *poor* as some of my other family members. I was better off than other people who didn't have new shoes or new clothes or didn't have access to some of the basic things that I had. This made me think I wasn't poor. It wasn't until I was an adult that I understood the failings of this country, not just for myself, but for the generations of my family that have existed in the desert southwest for generations, because while I share that I'm a fourth-generation

Mexican American, my family and my ancestors have been on this land for millennia.

I'm often asked how I became so politicized and whether incarceration influenced my views. I usually tell people my views, and being politicized came before imprisonment. I had the privilege of attending a magnet computer and science high school with people from across the county who were multiracial, with varying gender expressions, and came from working-class backgrounds. So, of course, the memories from the first grade with Mrs. Hara forced me to challenge my ideas about justice and fairness. My upbringing included interactions with medical professionals as they hosted free clinics, churches, and community centers, combined with waiting in line for free food and then having it all shift and change rapidly as I became a teenager. It was then I could understand the economic disparity, poverty levels, what makes an individual poor, as well as what pushes families into intergenerational poverty that denies them opportunities to expand their horizons or understand something different.

And, of course, my first year of high school wholly shaped that angst that was boiling in me that I didn't know what to do with. At the time, during an assembly to celebrate Christopher Columbus Day, the school invited a local nonprofit organization, a community-based group nearby, to address the students. Members of this group came in and started telling us the truth about Christopher Columbus. What he had done to Indigenous people, not just the colonization but the harm and the destruction that came with him and the individuals who traveled with him, gave me a whole new context. It made me question, along with many of my classmates, what was going on politically and what that looked like. We had been lied to for a long time, and this just further awakened me.

I am a kid who grew up benefiting from certain social safety nets, like summer lunch programs and summer activities that fed me and taught me skills. In addition, having significant amounts of privilege, I was going to this magnet school and being introduced to computer science before it was what it is today. Encouraged to think outside of what my family had known or been educated about really allowed me to grow and be the politicized person that I am. I'd also like to think that being on the debate team with a diverse group of people who discussed the failings of our society—from homelessness in the 1980s, which was centered on deinstitutionalization, to figuring out nuclear solutions, to healing our environment—I was wide awake at a very young age, before incarceration, about what fails us.

And last but not least, I knew I was queer at a very young age and fought hard to be accepted in this world—from having a new identity that was also marginalized to growing up seeing the literal hate to people watching MTV's *The Real World* with Pedro Zamora, an openly gay man who shared his struggle with HIV and AIDS, to just wanting to be accepted for who I was. Despite growing up in a fundamentalist Christian home that told me my sheer existence was a sin, these are the types of things that force folks not only to think outside of the box but to be unafraid and unwilling to compromise when it comes to how other people treat you, how you're respected, and where your dignity lies in as a person.

From being a six-year-old first-grader introduced to the suffering of somebody I cared about and respected as an educator, to gaining a deeper insight into what poverty looked like for poor, Black and Brown people, and immigrants, to having that awakening about the founding of this nation, to discovering my identity as a queer, and fighting to be accepted as someone different yet sharing the same core values as others in that time, I'm grateful that I was politicized and that this awakening reached me so early in life so that I could question everything which I did, which wasn't always the best or brightest move but it was my move nonetheless. My convictions wouldn't allow me to be silent about wrong things and adjust.

2
Gun Violence, A Night's Impact

Learning Objectives

1. Understand how intersecting identities shape the experiences of gun violence survivors.
2. Identify systemic flaws in the criminal justice system that hinder justice for marginalized communities.
3. Recognize the importance of community support in healing and empowering survivors of violent crimes.

> Pain and suffering are always inevitable for a large intelligence and a deep heart.
>
> —Fyodor Dostoyevsky, *Crime and Punishment*

To truly understand the impact of gun violence, one must delve into the lived experiences of survivors. The aftermath is not confined to physical wounds but extends to the intricate web of emotional, psychological, and societal repercussions. The scars of that fateful night stand as a testament to my personal resilience and as a mirror reflecting the urgent need for systemic change.

Like many Latinos, I grew up in the barrio. I was raised less than a mile from my mother's home in the east side's housing projects. I didn't know it was a rough neighborhood. Like most kids,

I was ordered back into my home when the streetlights came on at night. We had a yard filled with lemon and orange trees, a decent-sized garden, a swing set, and grapes. My maternal grandparents, both born in Texas, had moved to California to chase their dreams. I doubt they dreamed of farm labor, but that is what they did with pride.

I loved riding my bike in the neighborhood but often tried to avoid the alley behind my house. I feared it. Adults told us stories of crime, oftentimes in Spanish (which I did not speak as a child), as if they were shielding us kids from reality to the cars that raced down the alley with reckless abandon, and I was scared of it! Folks who emerged from this place on foot were foreign to me and always looked like they were up to no good. Feared it is more accurate!

It was a day like any other day. I woke up excited for summer break, made my bed, had cereal, and out of nowhere the impact of gun violence struck my young existence. On this day my friend Emilio, who was my neighbor's son, was shot while walking down this alley—a shortcut teenagers often took. I am unsure as to whether I heard the shot itself, or perhaps I did—it possibly sounded like a car backfiring or some other loud sound that radiated from the barrio, and this threw me off. I heard his screams. To this day, I will never forget him or the amount of blood there was. I immediately ran to tell my mother that Emilio, who was in the alley outside our garage, was shot. I don't think she believed me when I first said it until I pulled at her to see.

She immediately sent me to alert his mother to what had just happened. I will never forget what I saw next. His mother, Joanne, picked up her almost 15-year-old with herculean strength and ran down the street to the next block where our county hospital sat. Blood fell on the sidewalk all the way down the block. Had Joanne not run down the street—and I do mean a city block—he would not have made it. Ambulances rarely serviced our community, and together with the amount of blood I saw, I am sure he would have bled out. Now don't get me wrong. We often saw and heard ambulances speeding past our block to the hospital, but I do not recall any every being called to help my neighbors.

Emilio healed, but that day, I became keenly aware that my neighborhood wasn't safe. They never caught the person who did this to him. The police did eventually show up, and they treated us all like suspects, including my eight-year-old self. That was the day I learned to fear the police. And while I would have more events like this happen throughout my young life, this one hit home especially hard as Emilio and his older sister Alice often babysat me and my sister. We all grew up together. They were already living in the unit when we moved in, and their whole family welcomed us with open arms. Emilio was a trusted member of our extended family which was a hard thing to achieve.

Emilio was the older brother I never had, and he was just right on the other side of the wall in our duplex. If I looked out my window, I could see him practicing his pitch during baseball season. He loved baseball and had played as long as I can remember. He was good. Although he was older than me, he was my friend. I remember him at my fifth birthday busting my pinata and making sure us little kids got candy. He was kind and thoughtful. And while he did not die, he could have and that changed me.

Cannabis for Queers

In the early fall of 1994, the vibrant tapestry of San Francisco's Bay Area became the backdrop for my life. I had moved up there to attend college, and while most days I did, I relished in my new-found freedom and being able to love who I loved. I will never forget the first time I held a woman's hand in public. As I walked up University Boulevard holding her hand, I felt on top of the world. I did not grow up in a home that accepted what folks referred to as a "lifestyle." In fact, I grew up having attended the California church where Prop 8 would be born over a decade later.

Like many people, I relished my newfound freedoms. From late nights by the marina to all the raves and, of course, being a companion to my friends dying of AIDS. Oh, and let's not forget the culturally diversity that lit my heart on fire. I loved learning about other community's traditions and what they value. It was easy for me to see our intersectional needs, wants, and desires. Of course, like most of my life, I had to find places and spaces to be of service. Oakland had a radical history that I benefitted from, and I was eager to pay my homage and be of service. Oakland during that time felt like it was in perpetual punishment from the radical history of the Black Panthers. There were so many people with broken spirits, and the economic divide was painfully real. I could drive down Telegraph or San Pablo Boulevard and easily notice it.

One fateful afternoon while sitting in an apartment I shared with two friends from my hometown, a familiar face stopped by on their way to the city. We had a casual conversation about the weather, and I shared I was heading to the city to visit with a mutual friend. The delight in their eyes when I said that was a little uncomfortable for me as I knew something was up. They shared that they didn't have time to drop off something to our mutual friend and his roommate, and asked whether I could do it. That something happened to be a kilo of cannabis. You could imagine my shock at this request.

I was a hard *no way* until he shared with me that it was for my friend Kevin who I was scheduled to visit in an hour. At the time, Kevin had not shared his diagnosis with me. So, with a sense of urgency, I picked up the sack of weed and put in my Jansport backpack, holding onto the words of the friend who had asked for a favor, saying I looked white enough to go unbothered by law enforcement. The thoughts that raced through my head had nothing to do with whether this was right or wrong or if the cops were going to get me. Rather they were centered on the fact that my friend was going to most likely die, and he hadn't told me. Did he not trust me enough to share this news? Who was going to take care of him? I just wanted to hug him and tell him he wasn't alone and that I was here for him.

As I got off the BART (Bay Area Rapid Transit) and made my way to the street, the friend who said I looked white enough was right. Despite all the cops in the subway, not one of the stopped me or even looked my way. I made my way up the hill to Kevin's apartment that he shared with three other friends, all of whom had been kicked out of their homes from across the country because they were queer. While they were so creative and talented, their medical status combined with where we were as world relegated them to sex work. As I got closer to their apartment, I cried as I thought about what I would say.

When Kevin opened the door, he wasn't surprised to see me as I was expected that day; however, he was curious as to why was I there a little early. I opened my backpack, whipped out the giant sack of weed, and just hugged him. We cried for a while just holding each other like old friends do, even though we had known one another for less than six months. We spent the rest of the day focusing not on death but on life. We laughed and joked about how I, of all people—the good church girl who was afraid to jaywalk—had brought the weed into the city and broken the law. As I got ready to leave, one of the roommates pointed to money on the table and reminded me to take it. As I left, I grabbed the envelope and asked them who I should give this to. They laughed and teased me, by calling me church girl, and told me it was mine. The amount was more than what I made in a whole week at my internship.

Cannabis access during that time is not what it is today. As the epidemic ravaged LGBTQ+ populations, particularly gay men and transgender individuals, the lack of government response and the stigmatization of those affected highlighted deep-seated inequalities. The crisis exposed how systemic discrimination within the healthcare system and the broader society denied LGBTQ+ individuals essential medical care, resources, and support. Activism during this period, led by groups such as ACT UP, drew attention to the ways in which the criminalization of LGBTQ+ identities, through laws and social stigmas, compounded the community's vulnerability. This resulted in groups such as the Marijuana Buyer's Club being formed in the heart of San Francisco's Castro district. This activism not only fought for access to life-saving treatments but also challenged the criminal justice system's role in perpetuating violence and exclusion against LGBTQ+ people, thereby sparking broader debates about civil rights and social justice that continue to resonate today.

While the majority of my free time was devoted to supporting my siblings who were HIV positive or had AIDS, there were, on occasion, other much more financially lucrative opportunities to participate in this underground medical marijuana market. My heart and my commitment were to my friends with limited resources and access that would embarrass people in the cannabis market today. While the public face of compassionate cannabis was white, its redheaded step-sibling was filled with poorer people from all walks of life and all colors of the rainbow.

It was during this time that I began exploring ways to increase my contribution not only to my sick friends but to myself. I was no longer the naive person who had no idea I was getting paid to transport cannabis from point A to point B to help my friends. I now had access to large amounts of the product that I could sell outside of my community and still support my friends with free access. I made friends for life from this time. Those who lived and those I still get to honor today include the late Dennis Peron, a gay man who refused to see his partner die without dignity, and to him I am forever grateful.

Oakland: The Town

For a short time, I lived with one of my uncles and his wife. My mom's brother, Tio Jack, worked as a chef at UC Berkeley, while my aunt Julia was a nurse at Alta Bates Hospital. They were much older than my parents but provided me with enough freedom, guidance, and love to feel safe in the new space I occupied in the lower bottoms of West Oakland. They were the first to take me to a bar. As I was underage, they did not allow me to drink, but there was a Raider's game any my uncle had cooked some Pozole. Today that neighborhood is incredibly gentrified. Hell, the bodega on the corner sells my bougie overpriced Coconut Water from Thailand that I can't live without. But back then I was one of the whitest faces, and you could see the poverty all around the area despite my family being working middle class.

It wasn't until a musical artist from the group Tony! Toni! Toné! moved back into the neighborhood filled with Victorians that change could be seen. That was around the time I lived there. The block parties that were hosted during my first few months of living there were incredible. From the food to the music, it felt just like the monthly celebrations I had with my Tata in the housing projects but on steroids. Two and a half years spent navigating the streets of Oakland and experiencing the beauty of the region had opened my eyes to a world of transformation. It was a period marked by personal discovery—an unearthing of my identity outside the confines of my conservative Christian parents' home. Love, friendships, and a radical awakening inspired by the legacy of the Black Panthers defined this phase of my life.

Most of my love for "The Town," as it is commonly known, ended when an incident that would irreversibly alter the course of my life happened. Yet, amid the kaleidoscope of cultural richness, the mid-1990s in California presented a battleground for communities like mine. The era witnessed the implementation of the Crime Bill, the ominous Three Strikes law, a widening wealth gap, and the unsettling presence of the Ku Klux Klan at my first pride event in 1994. It felt like we were still living in the Wild West, navigating a landscape fraught with contradictions—lowriders and cruising being criminalized in my hometown and crime-ridden streets in Oakland. Little did I know that a nightmarish ordeal awaited me, shattering all illusions of security and freedom.

In the mid-1990s, California's landscape surrounding criminalization was marked by intense policing, racial disparities, and the implementation of harsh punitive measures. This period saw the height of the "War on Drugs," which disproportionately targeted Black, Indigenous, and People of Color (BIPOC) communities, particularly Black and Latino populations. I will never be able to unsee a sheriff's sub-station erected in the middle of the street in a friend's neighborhood for "safety reasons." The neighborhood looked dead; everyone avoided it like the plague. Ironically, at the same time, you could buy weed two streets away, where there was a line of people waiting to gain access. I was denied access just once cause of how white I looked. The guy got cussed out in Spanish as I walked away. The next time around, we laughed about it, and he started calling me Huera—a term meaning "light skinned" in Spanish.

The criminal justice system became a tool for enforcing racial segregation and economic disenfranchisement, contributing to mass incarceration. Laws such as the Three Strikes rule, enacted in 1994, mandated life sentences for repeat offenders and significantly increased the prison population. Hence, California was ostensibly the birthplace of the Prison Industrial Complex and across the country. In addition, LGBTQ+ individuals faced systemic discrimination and criminalization, particularly in relation to sodomy laws and police harassment. This environment laid the groundwork for ongoing struggles against racial and social injustices, with lasting effects on marginalized communities in California.

As states across the country adopted similar policies, the U.S. prison system expanded dramatically, with the number of incarcerated individuals rising from around one million in the early 1990s to over two million by the early 2000s. These laws disproportionately targeted Black, Latino, and low-income communities, leading to severe racial disparities in incarceration rates. The legacy of these policies entrenched a punitive approach to crime, perpetuating cycles of poverty, disenfranchisement, and systemic racial injustice that continue to affect marginalized communities today.

A Night's Impact

On returning from a successful trip to Seattle in 1997, where I facilitated underground cannabis transactions, my life took a dark and unforeseen turn. My arrival at the airport marked the beginning of a harrowing ordeal that would resonate far beyond the immediate physical and emotional trauma. While walking to my vehicle, something cold pressed against my back as I heard a chilling voice deliver the dreaded command: "Don't move." Familiar with the voice, I knew trouble awaited. With a gun to my back, he shuffled me into their car. A group of women, including his girlfriend and one person I vaguely knew and another I had never seen, waited in the car. We quickly drove off. They subjected me to a brutal assault, stole my belongings, and inflicted physical harm for over several hours.

The night unfolded in a series of dark streets and isolated locations. Forced to strip, I endured relentless physical attacks. The threat of a bleak future loomed until a security officer intervened, halting the assailants and potentially saving my life. The physical, mental, and emotional harm inflicted that night lingered, leaving scars that reached far beyond the visible bruises.

In the aftermath, seeking justice through law enforcement seemed futile. The code of the streets warned against cooperating with the police, and the prevailing sentiment was "snitches get stitches." Despite being a victim, pursuing medical attention, counseling, or support services felt unattainable. Fear gripped me; the perpetrators knew where I lived and who I loved.

This traumatic event left an indelible mark, triggering fear, anxiety, anger, and nightmares. Returning home, three and a half hours away from Oakland, I grappled with a newfound vulnerability.

The 1990s lacked victim advocacy programs and support organizations that are available today, thus leaving me to navigate the aftermath virtually alone. Although organizations existed at that time, the ones I would feel uncomfortable with were incredibly underfunded and grassroots. While I knew I had been harmed, I also knew I was involved in illegal activities unlike others or so I thought. I wasn't going to seek support from an organization with ties to law enforcement fearing further harm.

So, I did what anyone would do. I went home to my family to feel safe and secure. I took time for myself, which included taking long walks by the lake and spending more time with those who loved me. While it did not take away the pain, mentally

I felt that my bruises had healed; I felt more and more like myself in that safety net. My family encouraged me to not seek street justice and potentially put myself in harm's way again. I spent time in deep meditation and prayed for god or the universe to intervene and keep me safe as I had to return to my life in the bay.

Life as a Crime Survivor

Understanding the impact of gun violence on survivors is crucial. The trauma, emotional distress, and potential for post-traumatic stress disorder (PTSD) demand a new approach from institutions. While seeking mental health services and connecting with support groups can aid recovery, somebody must recognize the unique needs of queer BIPOC gun violence survivors.

The scars of that fateful night run deep, casting shadows on my sense of safety and trust. The trauma, both physical and psychological, wove through the fabric of my existence, leaving an indelible imprint on my outlook on life at the time. As I reflect on the events that unfolded, I was compelled to explore the personal ramifications and the societal undercurrents that allowed such an incident to occur. The inadequacies of the criminal justice system, the prevalence of violence, the code of the streets, and the lack of support systems require scrutiny.

In essence, this night forever altered my trajectory, forcing me to address the complexities of trauma, the inadequacies of the criminal justice system, and the crucial need for tailored support for survivors of violent crimes in real authentic ways. As my story unfolds, it intertwines personal experience with broader societal issues, setting the stage for a deeper exploration of the impacts of mass incarceration, policing, and the carceral state. I am just grateful to be one of those who gets to talk about it

The inadequacies of the criminal justice system became painfully apparent as I navigated the aftermath. The prevailing culture of silence, fueled by fear and mistrust, hindered any notion of seeking justice through conventional channels. "Snitches get stitches" echoed in my mind, reinforcing a chilling reality—cooperating with law enforcement seemed synonymous with placing a target on my back. The system, designed to protect, felt more like a labyrinth of inequity, especially for marginalized communities.

It became evident that support for survivors of gun violence, particularly queer BIPOC individuals, requires a comprehensive and culturally sensitive approach. Merely addressing the physical wounds is insufficient. The trauma, emotional distress, and potential for PTSD demand nuanced strategies that extend beyond conventional mental health services, requiring the community to think outside the textbook analysis.

Imagine a society where victim advocacy programs and support organizations bridge the gaps in the aftermath of violent crimes. Picture a landscape where fear of reprisal is replaced by a robust system that values justice, empathy, and healing. In this alternate reality, survivors don't face the daunting choice between silence and risking their lives by seeking justice. We are slowly moving in the needed direction. But America is incredibly slow on accountability and change.

As I grappled with the aftermath of that night, I longed for a support system that understood the intersectionality of my identity—a queer person of color navigating the impact of a violent crime. The challenges I faced extended beyond physical injuries; they delved into the complexities of mental health, the fear of retribution, and the lack of comprehensive resources.

My story unfolds not only as a personal testimony but also as a call to action. It beckons one to confront the inherent flaws in the criminal justice system and advocates for a paradigm shift toward a more equitable and victim/survivor-centered approach. My story transcends individual trauma, evolving into a broader exploration of systemic issues that perpetuate cycles of violence and hinder the healing process.

The scars on my body tell a tale of survival, but the tears on society's fabric beg for a collective reckoning. As the book navigates the intricacies of my journey, it seamlessly weaves into the broader context of societal challenges. It lays bare the inadequacies of a system that often fails to provide justice for victims, particularly those from marginalized communities. It is a system that prefers punishment and does not believe in redemption; but, I, along with a host of others, know better. We know what our community needs but, most importantly, what it deserves.

In the next chapters, we will delve deeper into the broader implications of mass incarceration, my subsequent incarceration, and the path less traveled to freedom.

3
Criminal Justice in California and Beyond

Learning Objectives

1. Understand how historical and political factors shaped the prison system in California.

2. Examine the role of racial and economic disparities in mass incarceration globally and in California.

3. Evaluate the impact of prisons on society and explore reform and abolition efforts.

The prison and jail system as we know it today is a relatively recent development in human history. Prisons were not originally intended to be long-term solutions for crime but rather places to hold individuals temporarily until their trial or punishment. In the eighteenth and nineteenth centuries, European penal reform movements, particularly in Britain and the United States, began promoting imprisonment as an alternative to corporal punishment or execution. The idea was to reform the criminal through confinement, which laid the groundwork for the modern penitentiary system.

In the United States, the first state prisons were built in the early nineteenth century based on models like the Pennsylvania and Auburn systems, which emphasized solitary confinement and labor as means of moral reform. However, these systems quickly became overcrowded and punitive, and moved away from their rehabilitative intentions. By the late nineteenth and early twentieth centuries, prisons had become institutions of punishment rather than reform—a trend that accelerated in the decades that followed.

In California, the state's prison system developed in the wake of the Gold Rush in the mid-1800s, with the opening of San Quentin State Prison in 1852 and Folsom State Prison in 1880. Both facilities were built to manage the influx of laborers and displaced people drawn by the gold economy, many of whom were criminalized for minor offenses. These facilities still exist today. Dilapidated. The early California prison system reflected broader U.S. trends of using incarceration as a tool for social control, especially for marginalized communities such as Indigenous peoples, Chinese immigrants, and Mexican laborers.

By the twentieth century, the United States had begun to industrialize its prison system. This coincided with increasing racial and economic inequalities, which became deeply embedded in law enforcement and judicial practices. The rise of "Jim Crow" laws in the South and discriminatory policing in the West and North led to disproportionate incarceration rates for Black and Latino communities.

In California, the prison population surged dramatically during the mid-twentieth century, particularly after the 1960s, as the state adopted "tough on crime" policies in response to social unrest and racial movements. The 1980s and 1990s saw the implementation of policies like the Three Strikes law, which disproportionately targeted Black and Latino individuals and resulted in life sentences for minor, nonviolent offenses. These laws, part of a national trend fueled by the War on Drugs, caused the prison population to skyrocket. Between 1980 and 2006, California's prison population grew by over 500 percent, becoming one of the largest prison systems in the world.

By focusing on punitive measures rather than addressing the root causes of crime—such as poverty, systemic racism, and lack of mental health services—California became a central player in the global rise of mass incarceration. This historical trajectory set the stage for the deeply entrenched system of racial and economic inequality that characterizes California's criminal justice system today.

Prisons and Jails as Part of a Larger Criminal Justice Issue in California and Beyond

California's prison and jail systems are not isolated entities; rather, they are deeply embedded within the larger global crisis of criminal justice, characterized by mass incarceration, racial disparities, and faulty systems that fail to address root causes of criminal behavior. The United States gifted this atrocity to the world. These issues are driven by sociopolitical dynamics that reinforce inequalities across racial, economic, and gender lines. By focusing on punishment and containment, rather than rehabilitation, justice systems worldwide have perpetuated cycles of poverty, violence, and disenfranchisement, particularly for marginalized communities. Michelle Alexander's work on the racialized nature of mass incarceration in the United States, especially in California, illustrates this phenomenon. She notes that "Black men are imprisoned at nearly six times the rate of white men" in the United States, largely due to policies like the War on Drugs (Alexander, 2010).

Across the world, prison populations have surged in recent decades, with many countries adopting increasingly punitive approaches to crime. The United States, and California specifically, has become a central example of this trend. California, home to one of the largest prison systems in the country, mirrors the national incarceration rate of 639 per 100,000 residents as of 2021—a figure that is significantly higher than most other nations. Ruth Wilson Gilmore emphasizes that the expansion of California's prison system was not simply a reaction to rising crime rates but was deeply connected to economic and political factors, such as surplus labor, land, and the decline of social safety nets. Governmental shifts toward "tough on crime" policies in the 1980s and 1990s fueled mass incarceration, particularly for communities of color, where poverty and social instability were criminalized rather than addressed (Gilmore, 2007).

This phenomenon is not limited to the United States. Globally, countries such as Brazil, Russia, and South Africa have experienced similar surges in incarceration, with prison populations exploding over the past two decades. For example, Brazil's prison population increased by over 167 percent between 2000 and 2020, contributing to severe overcrowding, inadequate healthcare, and ongoing human rights violations. Many of these prisons, like those in California, are notorious for poor living conditions, violence, and lack of rehabilitation programs. Overcrowding has also worsened the spread of diseases, including tuberculosis and HIV, in prisons across Brazil and Russia.

The rise in prison populations globally is deeply tied to cultural and economic factors. In many countries, punitive policies targeting marginalized groups—such as racial minorities, the poor, and political dissidents—have been enacted under the guise of maintaining social order. In Brazil, the War on Drugs has disproportionately affected Afro-Brazilian communities, just as California's policies have targeted Black and Latino populations. Angela Davis highlights that these incarceration trends often reflect a global culture of criminalizing poverty, where governments use imprisonment to manage social inequalities rather than address root causes such as unemployment, inadequate housing, and lack of mental health services (Davis, 2003).

Economically, the costs of mass incarceration are staggering. In California, the state spends over $13 billion annually on its prison system, diverting crucial resources away from education, healthcare, and housing. Similarly, in countries such as Brazil and South Africa, vast sums are spent maintaining expansive prison systems, often at the expense of social services. These economic priorities reflect a global trend where punitive systems are prioritized over social investment, leading to a cycle of dependency on incarceration to control marginalized populations.

Culturally, mass incarceration reinforces stigmas and perpetuates racial and economic inequalities. Incarcerated individuals, particularly from minority communities, are often viewed as inherently criminal, a narrative that echoes colonial-era beliefs about race and criminality. This stigma makes it difficult for formerly incarcerated individuals to reintegrate into society, exacerbating cycles of poverty and criminalization. In California, formerly incarcerated people face significant barriers to employment, housing, and social reintegration, with nearly two-thirds of those released returning to prison within three years, a pattern mirrored in many countries with high incarceration rates.

The global expansion of prisons has also been linked to broader economic trends, including neoliberalism and the privatization of prisons. In the United States, private prison corporations, driven by profit motives, have played a significant role in promoting policies that increase incarceration. This economic model has been exported to other countries, including the United Kingdom and Australia, where privatized prisons are becoming more common. The privatization of prisons incentivizes mass incarceration, as corporations benefit from higher prison populations, further entrenching a punitive approach to crime.

California's prison system serves as a microcosm of global incarceration trends, where cultural biases, economic interests, and political decisions have fueled the rise of punitive systems at the expense of addressing the root causes of social inequality. The global crisis of mass incarceration highlights the urgent need for reform, not only to alleviate overcrowded and inhumane conditions but also to shift away from a system that perpetuates cycles of violence, poverty, and disenfranchisement.

Disparities and Harm

One of the most striking elements of California's incarceration issue is the racial and economic disparity within prison populations. As Angela Davis (2003) highlights, systems of incarceration disproportionately target communities of color. In California, while African Americans make up just 6.5 percent of the state's population, they account for nearly 28 percent of the prison population. Similarly, Latinos are overrepresented, constituting approximately 40 percent of the prison population. This racial disparity reflects systemic racism that permeates law enforcement and judicial systems, leading to biased policing and sentencing practices.

These disparities are not unique to the United States. Loïc Wacquant's research demonstrates that globally, marginalized communities—such as Indigenous populations in Australia or Dalits in India—are often overrepresented in prison populations due to systemic oppression and economic inequalities (Wacquant, 2009). In California, socioeconomic inequalities intersect with race, as impoverished communities are disproportionately policed and punished for minor offenses linked to survival, such as drug possession or petty theft.

Prisons often serve as institutions of violence rather than rehabilitation. In California, with its notoriously overcrowded prison system—operating at 137% capacity as of 2019—incarceration exacerbates conditions like mental illness and substance abuse. According to a 2017 report, nearly 30 percent of California's prisoners required mental health services, but the majority do not receive adequate care (Gilmore, 2007). The situation is no better globally, as Wacquant (2009) illustrates, where prisons often worsen the mental and physical conditions of incarcerated individuals, creating environments where violence is both a survival mechanism and a systemic feature.

Prisons are often tools of social and economic control. Gilmore (2007) notes that California's prison boom paralleled the dismantling of social safety nets, with punitive policies such as the War on Drugs disproportionately targeting Black and Latino communities. Angela Davis (2003) expands on this, explaining that this pattern is evident globally, where governments often prioritize punishment over prevention, further entrenching social inequalities.

On a global scale, this trend is mirrored in countries such as the Philippines where the War on Drugs has led to mass imprisonment and extrajudicial killings, which are disproportionately affecting poor communities. In China, the incarceration of Uyghur Muslims under the guise of counterterrorism serves as another example of how prisons are used to control marginalized populations.

The Movement for Prison Abolition and Reform

California's ongoing prison closures, such as the California Correctional Center in Susanville, are part of a growing global movement toward prison abolition and reform. This movement challenges the efficacy of incarceration, promoting rehabilitation and community-based justice alternatives. Davis (2003) calls for a reimagining of the justice system, advocating for restorative justice approaches that prioritize healing over punishment. Globally, Norway's rehabilitation-focused prison system serves as a model, boasting one of the lowest recidivism rates at just 20 percent, compared to California's rate of over 65 percent within three years of release.

California's prison system is emblematic of a global crisis in criminal justice. By focusing on addressing root causes—poverty, systemic racism, and lack of mental health services—rather than punishment, societies can work toward a more just and equitable future. The prison abolition and reform movements remind us that real change requires dismantling the carceral system and investing in communities. As Gilmore (2007) and Alexander (2010) suggest, justice systems that prioritize human dignity, healing, and community empowerment can help break the cycles of incarceration and inequality.

4
Jail: A Walk on the Wild Side

Learning Objectives

1. Analyze the dehumanizing effects of the jail arrival process on individuals.
2. Critically evaluate systemic complexities within the criminal legal system.
3. Examine how poverty, race, and gender intersect in the context of incarceration.

> Jails and prisons are designed to break human beings, to convert the population into specimens in a zoo—obedient to our keepers, but dangerous to another."
>
> —Angela Davis

In the fall of 1997, my world turned topsy-turvy. An associate who owed me 100k at one point refused to pay. I had to push another associate, his boss, to clear the debt. So, you can understand my surprise and anger as this individual told me they were only going to be paying me only half of the debt they accrued and that I had to live with it. It wasn't just their refusal to pay me all they owed, but the nonchalant arrogance behind it. I was just a young queer woman, seen unworthy of receiving what was rightfully mine. While I regret the actions that came next, which subsequently led to my incarceration, I still stand by the fact that I have no tolerance for thieves. And this gentleman was a thief.

So, in all my wisdom at 21 and fueled by intense anger, I went to get my money. I had no real plan other than to let my weapon and the homeboy I hired to assist in obtaining the rest of my money do the trick. Little did I know that they would call law enforcement on me to shield themselves and that I would be staring down the barrel of a cop's gun. My co-defendant would get away that day but would later be arrested on other charges. I just wanted my money but got far more than I ever thought possible.

Arriving at a jail plunges one into an abyss of uncertainty and harsh realities. It's a journey that unfolds in stages—each step a descent into an environment designed to strip away personal belongings and the sense of self. This account delves deeper into the multifaceted experience of a person upon their arrival at a jail—examining the transition's physical, emotional, and psychological dimensions.

The initial encounter is a stark confrontation with the loss of personal autonomy. The process of being stripped, searched, and fingerprinted is more than a routine—it's a ritual that signals the beginning of a disorienting journey.

The act of disrobing extends beyond the physical removal of clothing; it's the stripping away of identity. Each layer shed represents not just fabric but the symbolic unraveling of the self. The starkness of the environment, coupled with the exposure to vulnerability, amplifies the feeling of powerlessness. "As layers of fabric fell away, so did my sense of self, exposing the vulnerability that would become the backdrop of my journey through the criminal justice system" (Felicia C., personal letter to family).

The room where one is sent after the physical stripping is an icy chamber, both in temperature and ambiance. Cold, sterile, and devoid of life, it sets the tone for what lies ahead. The institutional chill lingers, seeping into the individual's consciousness, foreshadowing the harsh realities of the confinement to come. The cold room wasn't just a space but a prelude to the isolation and detachment that would characterize my days behind bars. The chill mirrored the emotional freeze that awaited within those stark walls.

From the cold room begins a labyrinthine journey through the complex structure of the jail. The shuffle is not just a physical movement; it's a mental and emotional navigation through an unfamiliar and often dehumanizing terrain.

In Los Angeles County, sub-jails serve as temporary stops. These are places where one can't spend the night unless consigned to the drunk tank. The sub-jails initiate the process, setting the tone for the subsequent shuffling between institutions. Each stop adds another layer to the disorientation, making it challenging to grasp the contours of the more extensive system. The sub-jails introduced me to the disturbing narrative of the jail system. Each temporary stop brought a new cast of characters and a fresh wave of uncertainty, laying the foundation for the journey ahead.

Statistics

In 1997, the Los Angeles County jail system faced a considerable influx of women. Overcrowding was rampant, with sub-jails operating at capacity, exacerbating the already overburdened system. The transition from Sybil Brand Institute, a women's jail, to the Twin Towers Correctional Facility in the mid-1990s marked a significant shift in the landscape of incarceration in Los Angeles County. Sybil Brand Institute, which opened in 1963, was plagued with overcrowding, poor conditions, and lack of adequate resources. These issues, combined with a growing jail population and rising public scrutiny, led to its closure in 1997.

The opening of Twin Towers Correctional Facility in 1997, touted as a modern solution to the existing problems in prisons, was one of the largest and most technologically advanced jails in the world at the time. Designed to house over 4,000 prisoners, Twin Towers was intended to alleviate the overcrowding issue and provide better facilities, including medical and mental health services. However, the transition revealed deeper systemic problems within the Los Angeles County jail system.

Despite its state-of-the-art design, Twin Towers quickly became a symbol of the mass incarceration crisis, particularly for mentally ill prisoners. The facility was soon operating beyond its intended capacity, and the same issues of overcrowding, violence, and inadequate mental health care persisted, exacerbating the conditions prisoners faced. The jail's location in downtown Los Angeles, along with its imposing, fortress-like architecture, further reflected the punitive nature of the criminal justice system, where incarceration was favored over community-based solutions and rehabilitation.

The racial disparities in incarceration rates, particularly among Black and Latino communities, continued unabated, with the Twin Towers becoming another cog in the broader machinery of systemic racism and criminalization in Los Angeles County. The facility's inability to address the root causes of crime, such as poverty, mental illness, and substance abuse, meant that it served more as a warehouse for marginalized individuals rather than a center for rehabilitation and reintegration. While the move from Sybil Brand to Twin Towers was meant to improve conditions within Los Angeles County's jail system, it ultimately reinforced the challenges of mass incarceration, reflecting the broader issues of racial inequity and the criminalization of poverty and mental illness that defined the era.

Lucky me! I had the chance to be part of the very first class of residents. For some, like myself, the journey led to Twin Towers— a behemoth institution with an intricate maze of corridors and cells. My arrival there, as part of the first group of women directly sent, amplified my sense of being lost in a system designed to overwhelm. Twin Towers, an imposing labyrinth, greeted us with its towering walls, which echo the vastness of the challenges faced by those within. As part of the first group of women ushered in, the scale of the institution mirrored the enormity of the challenges that awaited us. It wasn't just a physical space but a manifestation of the systemic complexities that defined my days behind bars.

In 1997, the Twin Towers Correctional Facility in Los Angeles County witnessed a surge in the number of incarcerated women. Overcrowding and the institution's sheer scale added complexity layers to an already disorienting arrival process.

I had never shared this kind of space with women. I have 72 first cousins and a large extended family, but I have only one sister. I had gone to church camp and was housed with other women, but not this many. So, this amount of estrogen mixed with loss and deep sadness was riveting. There were so many poor people who had made poor choices—but not the kind you'd expect would land someone in jail or on the path to prison. The majority of women in the pod had experienced some kind of violent crime.

Many women were there for defending their bodies or selling their bodies in order to provide for their families. The primary drivers of crime were deeply rooted in the systemic issues of poverty, drug addiction, and the criminalization of survival behaviors, particularly among women of color. Some of the most significant factors and causes of arrests for women during this period are discussed below.

Drug-Related Offenses

The War on Drugs disproportionately affected women, particularly those from marginalized communities. Many women were arrested for drug possession, often tied to addiction. These arrests frequently stemmed from broader social issues like poverty, trauma, and lack of access to mental health services. The crack epidemic was at its height, and marijuana was enough to get you locked up.

Prostitution and Sex Work

Many women were arrested for prostitution-related offenses, a reflection of the criminalization of sex work and survival behaviors. These arrests were often linked to broader issues of economic vulnerability, exploitation, and trafficking, with limited support for women trying to escape these circumstances. Although today we acknowledge that sex work is work, this has not always been the case, and many women were incarcerated after repeated arrests.

Domestic Violence and Self-Defense

Women who were survivors of domestic violence often found themselves criminalized when defending themselves against their abusers. The criminal justice system frequently fails to recognize the context of self-defense, leading to arrests and incarceration for assault or related charges. I knew over a dozen women who were incarcerated for defending their children and themselves from their husbands or partners.

Property Crimes

Economic hardship led many women to engage in petty crimes such as theft or shoplifting. These acts were often driven by the need to provide for themselves or their children in the face of systemic poverty and limited economic opportunities. I would later have a roommate who was incarcerated for stealing baby food, diapers, and food during their addiction. She just wanted to feed her children. My heart still hurts from this reality as her children were later placed in Los Angeles' foster care system.

Parole and Probation Violations

Many women were incarcerated due to technical violations of parole or probation conditions rather than new criminal offenses. This could include missing a meeting with a parole officer, failing a drug test, or other minor infractions, which disproportionately affected women with unstable housing or ongoing addiction issues.

These factors highlight the intersection of gender, race, and economic inequality in the criminal justice system during this period. The conditions and policies that led to the incarceration of women at the Twin Towers often ignored the underlying social issues and instead opted for punitive measures that perpetuated cycles of incarceration. Women were at the bottom of the totem pole and, as always, were expected to act with dignity and grace; oftentimes, they were punished even more severely for not complying.

I had never shared my space with so many poor people. Sure, I visited the projects often, and sure, I had a large, primarily low-income family, but this was a different kind of poor. This was a poor that felt hopeless—a poor that made getting locked up and having a place to rest your head and three meals a day look good to some folks. A poor that gave women limited opportunities to not be victimized or criminalized. It was as if it was easier just to round women up and separate them from their children and force everyone into statistics than deal with root causes.

Within the walls of the jail, a dehumanizing routine unfolds—a series of actions that desensitize both the staff and the incarcerated.

The routine includes repeated strip searches, each instance a violation of personal boundaries. It's a process that erodes any remaining semblance of privacy, reducing individuals to mere bodies subjected to scrutiny. The frequency of these searches contributes to normalizing vulnerability, numbing both the searcher and the searched.

Stripped of dignity, the constant searches were a grim reminder that privacy was a luxury lost. The ritualized invasion blurred the lines between personhood and object, numbing both the enforcer and the enforced. I hated it there! I was angry with myself for putting myself in this position.

With its air of coldness and detachment, the institutional environment fosters a different kind of desensitization. The pain and suffering of individuals become routine occurrences, blurring the line between humanity and institutional indifference. The journey through this desensitization amplifies the trauma, creating an environment where empathy struggles to survive. Within those cold walls, suffering became a backdrop—an everyday occurrence the system learned to overlook. The desensitization to human anguish echoed the broader dehumanization embedded in the structures of incarceration.

Reports from 1997 highlight the prevalence of strip searches in the Los Angeles County jail system, emphasizing the routine nature of these invasive procedures. The environment's desensitization contributes to a culture where the suffering of prisoners is overlooked. Strip searches were conducted routinely on prisoners as part of the intake process, after visits, or whenever jail staff deemed it necessary. For women, these searches were particularly traumatic, as many had histories of sexual abuse or trauma. The routine nature of these searches, often conducted without clear justification, contributed to a culture of humiliation and powerlessness among the incarcerated population.

The strip search practices in Los Angeles County jails drew legal challenges and public outcry. One of the most notable cases was Edith H. *v.* County of Los Angeles (1997), in which the plaintiffs argued that the strip searches conducted on women in the jail system were unconstitutional and violated their Fourth Amendment rights. The case highlighted how these searches were often carried out in a degrading manner, sometimes in the presence of male guards, and without any individualized suspicion.

The environment within the Los Angeles County jail system, characterized by the desensitization of both staff and prisoners to such invasive practices, contributed to a broader culture where the suffering of prisoners was routinely overlooked. The normalization of strip searches and other harsh treatment reinforced the idea that prisoners, particularly women, were less deserving of dignity and respect. This culture of disregard for prisoners' humanity had lasting effects on those incarcerated, exacerbating trauma and undermining the possibility of rehabilitation.

Reports from this period, including investigations by civil rights organizations and journalists, further emphasized the systemic nature of these issues. The American Civil Liberties Union (ACLU) and other advocacy groups documented numerous cases of abuse within the Los Angeles County jail system, including the use of strip searches, and called for reforms to protect prisoners' rights.

Overall, the use of strip searches in Los Angeles County jails in the 1990s exemplified the broader issues of dehumanization and mistreatment that plagued the system. These practices were not only a violation of basic human rights but also a reflection of the deep-seated problems within a system that prioritized control and punishment over care and rehabilitation. They would make whole pods, a dorm that housed 50+ people. While women were the ones in the area, male Correctional Officers could easily still see the entire process.

Transportation within Justice Institutions

The journey continues with a bus ride to court—an uncertain expedition into the external world. The restraints, both physical and psychological, intensify the sense of vulnerability. The use of shackles on ankles and wrists symbolizes the loss of freedom. The interconnection of restraints amplifies the feeling of entrapment. Mobility is reduced to a shuffle—a symbolic representation of the constrained agency within the criminal justice system and the ever-growing tightening grip of loss. Shackled and bound, the bus ride to court was more than a physical journey; it was a met-aphor for the ride within the institutions I would take. I hated it. The shuffle became a dance of constraint—a stark reminder that freedom was a distant memory. I felt like I was being hog tied, just as I had once seen before an annual pig roast.

Arriving at court involves yet another shuffle, into old, neglected rooms, which added to the disorientation. The space becomes a character in this narrative, with its cold, often smelly, and uncared-for atmosphere. The feeling of dirtiness is all around you even though you know somebody had to have cleaned it or at least was paid to do so. The interaction with legal representatives and the judicial process unfolds in a surreal environment, isolated from the outside world. The courtroom shuffle was a dance of disarray, set against the backdrop of neglected rooms and the lingering scent of despair and old. I don't know whether it was old books or just the lack of care, but it reminded me of a convalescent home's odor. Legal interactions unfolded in a disconnected realm, far removed from the vibrancy of the world left behind.

Arriving at a jail is an inescapable reality—one that thrusts individuals into a disorienting whirlwind of physical and emotional stripping, navigating complex institutions, and confronting dehumanizing routines. The journey's impact extends beyond the physical boundaries of the jail, leaving an indelible mark on the psyche. The transition is more than a relocation; it's a descent into an environment designed to erase personal agency and reinforce institutional control.

I couldn't tell you who was in court or how many people were there. I barely remember the stenographer and other courtroom staff whose gaze often felt empty. It was as if they knew I was a bad person and that this formality needed to move swiftly so they could make whatever quota they had for the day. The sheriff deputies always had a much more pleasant demeanor, as if they were having fun. The formal yet simple shuffling process (be it public defenders, the criminal defense attorneys, or the defendants) was so odd to me.

Society places a lot of importance on individuals who work in the legal profession: one is required to go to law school, get your degree, pass the bar, and practice law. And while all the public defenders (often the only choice for poor people) did get their degrees, passed the bar, and were practicing law, they didn't appear to know much about the individual they were representing. For many, it felt like assembly line justice. The public defender was merely relaying information from the prosecutor's office or translating the judge. They often believed that their clients were terrible from the beginning and almost deserving of the punishment they received—at least, this was the sentiment of the many individuals I encountered.

One often goes to court multiple times. For example, if your court-appointed lawyer runs late in another courtroom, you just get bumped., Basically, this means that you went through the process for nothing—no date closer to a trial or taking a plea. You just got a free trip out of jail into the whatever of going to court without actually going to court. I knew so many people who experienced such false starts. All too often, these added to the discontent of people who just wanted justice, even if that justice led them to a prison sentence.

5
A-Yard

Learning Objectives

1. Explore the challenges of transitioning from jail to state prison.
2. Evaluate disparities within the prison system based on gender expression and identity.
3. Understand mechanisms of community-building and resilience within carceral spaces.

> Prison is a second-by-second assault on the soul, a day-to-day degradation of the self. An oppressive steel and brick umbrella that transforms seconds into hours and hours into days.
>
> —Mumia Abu-Jamal

The transition from jail to state prison is a journey few discuss—a process as traumatizing as the experiences leading up to it. Understanding these differences is crucial for grasping how the California penal system functions and how individuals are processed through the criminal legal system depending on the severity of their charges and the length of their sentences. When we talk about bureaucracy and institutionalization, this serves as a prime example.

In the California penal system, jails and prisons serve distinct roles in the administration of "justice," each with specific functions, populations, and management structures. One of the most significant distinctions is the length of incarceration. Jails are intended for short-term stays, while prisons handle long-term sentences. Jails are managed locally and are under the jurisdiction of county or city authorities, while prisons are state or federally managed institutions. Jails often have a more transient population due to the mix of pretrial detainees and individuals serving short sentences. In contrast, prisons house individuals who have been convicted and are serving longer sentences, often for more severe offenses.

To explain further, jails are locally operated facilities typically managed by the county sheriff's department or the city police. They primarily house individuals who are awaiting trial and have not yet been convicted of a crime. These individuals are either unable to post bail or are denied bail based on the severity of their charges or because they are perceived as a risk. Jails also incarcerate individuals convicted of misdemeanors or minor felonies, usually serving sentences of one year or less. Jails are typically located within the county where the crime occurred, allowing easier access to court proceedings and legal counsel for the detained individuals.

Prisons, on the contrary, are state or federally operated institutions that handle longer-term incarceration. Prisons house individuals convicted of more serious crimes, particularly felonies, and they serve longer sentences, typically over one year. These facilities are designed to accommodate the needs of long-term imprisonment, offering various security levels—from minimum to maximum—to address the different risks posed by the prison population. In California, state prisons are operated by the California Department of Corrections and Rehabilitation (CDCR). Federal prisons, which house individuals convicted of federal crimes, are managed by the Federal Bureau of Prisons (BOP).

My crime was a state crime. So, I was sentenced to a state prison.

However, amid the trauma, there was a silver lining—the opportunity to witness the world beyond prison walls and breathe non-stale or recycled air. Natural air that doesn't carry the sterile scent of a hospital with the whiff of stale but rather the chilling freshness of freedom.

Having resolved to accept my guilt after navigating the intricate court process, I sought an expedited journey to prison, a place where I would no longer need to fight or endure endless lines alongside individuals deeply entrenched in their pain and trauma, often resorting to numbing substances to cope. Or so I thought from what I was told. Boy, were we wrong!

The decision to accept a deal, albeit unfair, led to my swift relocation within a couple of months. Picked up and transported to the new institution, the bus ride was not the liberating experience one might anticipate. It was a forced drive in silence, in which I was shackled and accompanied by an officer armed with a loaded gun.

Arriving at the Southern California A-Yard Reception Center at Central California Women's Facility (CCWF) in Chowchilla, the welcome was far from warm. Another round of strip searches awaited, followed by the receipt of essential state-issued items and then the journey to A-Yard. This area continued to be referred as the R&R. Not the kind associated with recreation. Still, it was one dedicated to further processing of a prisoner—a place where women received essential items such as underwear, bras, and the infamous muumuu.

The muumuu, traditionally a loose-fitting, flowing dress from Hawaiian culture, is often associated with femininity and comfort. I loved seeing my Polynesian friends wear them when I was a child. The stories they would share during cookouts at my grandfather's made me aware of their existence. We also had these garments in Mexican culture, but I resisted, with all my might for most of my life, wearing a dress despite how cute I looked.

When adapted as a prison garment, it carries different connotations. For genderqueer individuals—those who exist outside the binary of male and female—the muumuu can evoke mixed feelings, laughs, and discomfort in those moments that can be triggering for some of us. The imposition of the muumuu as a prison garment can also feel like a form of forced gender expression, mainly if it is intended to feminize or humiliate the wearer, often targeting those whose gender identity does not align with traditional norms. I experienced this over and over again.

From a genderqueer perspective, *my* perspective at the time, the muumuu in prison was a reminder of how institutional settings often enforce harmful stereotypes and erasures of *nonnormative* identities. This misuse strips the muumuu of its cultural roots and potential for gender inclusivity, turning it into an instrument of control rather than an expression of identity.

The state-issued clothing, consisting of basic jeans and a baseball T-shirt, fell short of expectations—often stained and worn by previous occupants. Navigating this environment, particularly for someone with an androgynous gender expression, proved challenging. An ill-fitting pale blue shirt added to the absurdity. I am approximately six feet tall and have a long torso, making this shirt a midriff style you would never see me wear—not even on a dirty laundry day.

The concept of "state property" became apparent. Everything in the room, including myself, belonged to the state. Damaging state property was strictly forbidden. I remember one instance where I got a sunburn as I worked outdoors in the sun and was threatened to get written up for damaging state property by an officer. These ideas were always wild to me. Becoming state property was never discussed when I took my plea deal. Being state property was something that is rarely talked about outside of the walls.

The phrase "property of the state or state property" is not a legally accurate or official designation but rather a rhetorical expression reflecting the prisoner's perception of status under incarceration. Legally, prisoners are not considered a "property" of the state in the literal sense. However, the phrase can be understood in key legal and conceptual contexts. First, you experience a loss of certain rights and liberties that you are reminded of by overzealous correctional officers daily.

When a person is incarcerated, they are subjected to a significant loss of personal freedoms and autonomy. The state controls many aspects of our lives, including movement, daily activities, and communication. This extensive control can lead prisoners to feel as though they are owned or possessed by the state, despite the fact that legally they remain individuals with certain protected rights. The state has legal custody and authority over prisoners through its prison system. This includes providing for their basic needs, enforcing rules, and maintaining order. While the state has this authority, it also has a legal duty to uphold the constitutional rights of prisoners, such as the right to be free from cruel and unusual punishment (Eighth Amendment), access to the courts (Fourteenth Amendment), and due process.

Historically, the notion of prisoners as "property" has dark roots in practices such as slavery and indentured servitude, where individuals were legally considered property. While these practices have been abolished, remnants of this language and sentiment can still appear in modern-day incarceration, especially in how prisoners might express their lack of autonomy. The phrase also reflects the dehumanizing effects of imprisonment, where prisoners often feel stripped of their individuality and reduced to a number or object under the state's control. This feeling can be exacerbated by the way the prison system operates, where personal identity is often suppressed in favor of institutional order.

I was W#72703

Living conditions in the shared cell for eight people lacked privacy—an oversight nobody had prepared me for. When I was younger, I had shared a bedroom with my younger sister; later, I had my own room. My room was was half the size of this eight-man cell, and I couldn't fathom having three other people in my room with me. Outside of my immediate family, I cannot recollect ever having more than three people in my room at once. I rarely let houseguests share the room with me. How could anyone be prepared for living like this? I did not understand how these institutions functioned or that I would one day work at the laundry, ensuring state-issued clothing was cleaned and issued in a controlled manner.

Reception centers at women's institutions emerged as unique worlds—a subhuman existence within a subhuman space. In the rare instances when we could go outside, we shared the yard with individuals in administrative segregation, including those on death row. Their movement froze the entire yard, forcing everyone to the ground. A-Yard, an extension of incarceration, revealed a harsh truth—the journey was getting worse.

Diving Deeper with Statistics

The statistics surrounding the journey through the California prison system in 1997 provide a stark backdrop to my narrative. In that year, CDCR reported alarming figures as the state prison population surged, reaching unprecedented levels.

Women, a minority within this vast system, faced unique challenges. The CCWF struggled with overpopulation. Reports indicated that many women's institutions, including Chowchilla, were stretched beyond capacity.

Administrative segregation, where individuals on death row often found themselves, created an atmosphere of heightened tension. The strained conditions affected yard time, limiting the moments of respite for incarcerated individuals.

The concept of "state property" resonated with the overarching theme of the prison-industrial complex for me. The prison population boom in the 1990s, driven by policies like the Three Strikes law, reflected a punitive approach that prioritized incarceration over rehabilitation. The disparities in treatment based on gender expression and identity became evident. In a system lacking sensitivity to diverse experiences, individuals with nonbinary identities were compelled to conform to rigid gender norms in their dress code, which further diminished their sense of agency.

The prevalence of forced silence during transportation and the impact of shackling (wrists, ankles, and belly chains) on individuals' mental well-being underscored the dehumanizing aspects of the criminal justice system. These statistics serve as a chilling backdrop to the personal narrative, thus emphasizing the urgent need for reform within the prison system.

Beyond the confines of the cell, I familiarized myself with the art of "fishing" and "kites." Kites were letters passed between prisoners, by forming a network to ensure messages reached their intended recipients. Fishing, the sport of shooting items under the door to another room, became a means of acquiring necessities like cookies or pencils. This was how we built community— trusting someone would pass a message to a cherished friend. You could see in the eyes of participants that this was an exciting albeit odd way to bond, and we bonded all the same.

6
Just a Bunch of Bad Girls

Learning Objectives

1. Examine the classification system within California prisons.
2. Evaluate systemic disparities and injustices within the prison system.
3. Reflect on the role of personal narratives in advocating for justice reform.

Amid the California prison yard in the 1990s, I encountered many women experiencing the complexities of incarceration. Our stories, like many, were woven into the fabric of an institution that stripped away our identities and freedoms. The system had labeled me as a high-security offender, a classification rooted in the crime I committed, leading me to the unexpected confines of the Central California Women's Facility (CCWF), the California Institute for Women (CIW), and the Valley State Prison for Women (VSPW).

The classification process in California prisons is complex and multifaceted, aiming to balance the goals of safety, security, rehabilitation, and individual needs of prisoners while incarcerated. That being said, it is frequently a score based on a rubric that analyzes factors such as the nature of one's crime, behavior within the institution, and other individual characteristics. One of the most significant factors is one's custody level: prisoners are often classified into different custody levels based on the seriousness of their offense and their potential risk to themselves, other prisoners, and staff. The custody levels typically range from Level I (minimum security) to Level IV (maximum security).

Work assignments are a key part of the CDCR prison system. Many incarcerated individuals are assigned jobs that contribute to the operation of the facility or broader state needs, such as maintenance, food service, manufacturing, or firefighting. Participation in these work assignments is often tied to prisoners' privileges, housing status, and sentence reduction opportunities. A prisoner refusing to participate in a work assignment without a valid reason (such as a medical condition) can lead to disciplinary action.

One of the most significant consequences is being placed on "C-over-C" status, "Confined to Quarters," which severely restricts the prisoner's movement and activities within the facility. Prisoners on C-over-C status lose many privileges typically available to those who comply with work requirements. They are generally confined to their cells during work hours, which can mean limited access to recreational time, educational programs, and social interaction. This status is intended to pressure prisoners into participating in work assignments by making nonparticipation uncomfortable and isolating.

Being on C-over-C status can also affect a prisoner's classification and parole prospects, as it reflects negatively on their behavior record. It underscores the prison system's emphasis on compliance and participation in institutional labor to maintain order and control within the facility. I was sentenced to do 85 percent of my sentence, so good time did not apply. I wanted to work out of sheer boredom, but knew that one day a situation might arise that I would have to do so because of the job or other underlying factors.

In 2024, California voters will decide whether the practice of forced labor, often referred to as slavery by activists challenging unfair wages, should be banned. May this former slave's wildest dream come true and we win this measure; hopefully, other states will follow suit.

Upon hitting the yard, I was thrust into a space reminiscent of a college campus—an *old* one, a dilapidated reminder of institutional neglect. This would be the first of many challenges I would face while incarcerated. I was not supposed to be at CIW, the oldest women's institution in California. While it was in Southern California where my crime occurred, I had only distant relatives nearby and no idea how they would send me there to train for a fire camp of all places when I would never be eligible for gate clearance outside of the institution.

Women's fire camps in California are specialized correctional facilities where incarcerated women are trained and deployed as firefighters to assist with wildfire suppression efforts. Operated by the CDCR in collaboration with the California Department of Forestry and Fire Protection (Cal Fire), these camps offer rigorous training to prisoners, equipping them with skills in firefighting, emergency response, and land management. The work is physically demanding and often dangerous, as these women work on the front lines alongside professional firefighters.

While the program provides valuable training, a sense of purpose, and the potential for sentence reductions, it is also controversial. The women are paid only a few dollars a day for their labor, raising ethical concerns about the exploitation of incarcerated workers. Moreover, despite the extensive experience gained, many face significant barriers to employment as firefighters after their release due to the stigma of a criminal record and specific licensing restrictions. Even today, with California state policies removing the barrier and providing pathways, it is still a one-in-a-million shot for someone with a record to actually find work in this field.

I was not going to risk my life to fight a fire even if I had qualified. All I remember thinking was that the state of California was crazy to think I would risk dying for pennies on the dollar, snacks, or some nature at a camp. I did not think of the potential experience as a luxury as the other ladies did. This was also before the state had added rehabilitation to its name—I did not and do not trust the Department of Corrections.

Despite the physical environment, CIW became a canvas where my journey toward compassion and self-discovery began. I remember sitting at my first classification with institution staff and the lieutenant stating, "Carbajal you shouldn't be here." I shared how I was fully aware I should not be there from the moment I was forced to put on another muumuu and get on a bus for the five-hour-long ride and how I was told to shut up every time I brought up the error. When I asked who I should submit a grievance report to regarding the inconvenience, they all just laughed.

On the upside, it prompted the lieutenant to look at me differently. She asked whether I wanted to work for her. She even called me *Mija*—a term of endearment in Spanish that often means "daughter." Although she was compassionate and funny as hell, I still saw her as a cop. But her benevolence and general interest in me could be felt at that table during my classification.

Being assigned to an institutional-need position granted me privileges—a stark contrast to the majority serving life sentences alongside me. An *institutional-need job* within California prisons refers to work assignments given to incarcerated individuals that are essential for the daily operation and maintenance of the prison facility. These jobs are crucial for keeping the prison running smoothly and include various tasks supporting the institution's essential functions. Overall, institutional-need jobs are a vital part of the California prison system, benefiting the facility's operation and thus saving the institution money while exploiting the prisoners who perform these essential tasks as cheap labor.

Prisoners may be assigned several jobs that meet institutional needs, such as cleaning common areas, cells, bathrooms, and administrative offices. This ensures the facility remains sanitary and safe for prisoners and staff. Many prisoners work in the prison kitchen, preparing, cooking, and serving meals to the entire prison population. These roles include cleaning the kitchen and dining areas and managing food inventory. Prisoners assigned to laundry duties are responsible for washing, drying, and folding the clothing and linens used by other prisoners and staff. There is also maintenance work such as plumbing and electrical. My assignment fell into the clerical work category. As I had suitable skills, I was chosen for a clerical position, which involved administrative tasks such as filing, data entry, or assisting prison staff with office work.

The pay is generally minimal, reflecting the prison system's broader use of prison labor. Consistent and positive performance in these jobs can lead to additional privileges, such as access to better housing units, increased visitation rights, or eligibility for other programs. Conversely, refusing to work or performing poorly can result in disciplinary action or loss of privileges. A prisoner's participation in institutional-need jobs is recorded and can positively impact their classification status and parole prospects. Demonstrating a willingness to work and good behavior through these assignments is often viewed favorably during parole hearings and other evaluations.

While I did not think a clerical job was as much of an institutional-need position as, say, a being cook or working at the laundry, I was happy to be in a somewhat cushy job that had this classification probably because I was working for the Lieutenant of Housing and Assignments, an office that ostensibly ensured the institution functioned to its full potential. While I did not have any special privileges other than being able to move into any unit or a room of my liking, the position had some perks. It was better than being forced to work a double shift as a cook or working as part of the yard crew in the summer heat (which I did one summer).

While my classification hinted at a short stint within CIW, I enjoyed the little freedom this provided me. The deep conversations I was afforded with so many women battling demons I could not understand was like diving into a real-life sociology class. From being in the yard with the Manson girls to conversations with so many women who defended their lives and killed someone (often a man/their abuser) to moms battling addiction—I saw it all.

Yes, I said Manson, as in the infamous Charles Manson. The Tate murders, which occurred on the night of August 8–9, 1969, are among the most infamous and brutal crimes in American history. Orchestrated by Charles Manson, members of his "Family"— including Charles "Tex" Watson, Susan Atkins, Patricia Krenwinkel, and Linda Kasabian—invaded the Los Angeles home of actress Sharon Tate, who was eight months pregnant at the time.

The LaBianca murders occurred on August 10, 1969, when members of Charles Manson's "Family" brutally murdered Leno and Rosemary LaBianca in their Los Angeles home. This attack came just one day after the infamous Tate murders, and both incidents were part of Manson's plan to incite a race war he dubbed "Helter Skelter." The LaBiancas were selected at random by Manson, who accompanied his followers to the house but did not participate in the killings himself. Instead, he commanded his followers—Charles "Tex" Watson, Patricia Krenwinkel, and Leslie Van Houten—to carry out the gruesome stabbings, leaving the couple dead and their home defaced with messages written in the victims' blood. The LaBianca murders, like the Tate killings, shocked the nation and became symbolic of the violent, cult-driven terror associated with the Manson Family.

Charles Manson's female co-defendants were often referred to as the "Manson Girls" due to their close association with Manson and their involvement in the crimes he orchestrated. The term "Manson Girls" emerged in the media and public discourse during and after the infamous trials of the late 1960s and early 1970s. This label reflected their cult-like devotion. The women, including Susan Atkins, Patricia Krenwinkel, and Leslie Van Houten, were part of the "Manson Family," a group of followers who lived communally and were deeply influenced by Manson's charismatic yet manipulative leadership.

I will never forget meeting Susan Atkins. I didn't know who she was, nor did I care. I was more interested in how peculiar she was. She was wearing biker shorts, which were out of style to me, and sporting a homemade necklace. While not odd on its own, this necklace was made of yarn strung with a half shell of a walnut with a handmade wooden cross in it. When I asked her what it was, she said, "Jesus in a nutshell, silly." The next day, while talking to my co-workers about housing and assignments, I found out who she was. To me, she just seemed odd.

I would go on to meet others in the Manson Family who did not communicate with one another and seemed to be adjusting to their fate like everyone else. They were not the only women convicted of murder; I learned this as one of my first assignments was to black out prisoner's conviction on their physical bed card. In those analog days, a bed card moved with each individual so Housing and Assignments could record their CDCR custody number, type of crime committed, housing unit, and work assignment. Thankfully this task became redundant due to digitization.

But nothing good lasts forever, and within nine months, I was sent back to an institution that supported my custody level and was closer to my family so I could have visits. The fact that I was leaving behind some of the luxuries and friendships I had found during my time at CIW saddened me. However, I was also grateful to be getting away from some of the bad influences I had met; these individuals, owing to their pain, sought solutions that were not rooted in the values I wanted to espouse. CIW was called Camp Snoopy across the state. It had trees and freedoms, which I was preparing to miss. The week I found out I was leaving, I hugged every tree and bought the maximum amount of all the canteen items that were not offered where I was going— both for bartering and for myself.

The Valley State Prison for Women, Chowchilla, California (Now Called the Valley State Prison for Men)

So, it was no surprise that I would find myself back in Central California, where I had the opportunity to connect with incredible souls, most notably Myra, a shy girl, whom I met during my stay there. And while I had been at the institution for several years before meeting and living with her, our paths were destined to cross. Her journey mirrored mine in unexpected ways. Incarcerated at 17 to two life sentences, she grappled with the fallout of trusting her gang when they assured her leniency due to her age. We both grew up in poor Latino homes. We were naive, well her more than me, and go so close that we would finish another's sentence; so much so that she she felt like family. Our favorite color was black; we loved Morrisey and pizza.

We hated the loudness of prison. We hated that people did not understand us or judged us just based on how we presented. In these shared struggles, our bond deepened.

She shared her experience with navigating this system, finding it laughable at times, with unclear messages and constant WTF moments. She talked about how jail was and how everyone kept telling her that she looked so innocent—something I was familiar with. She expressed feeling betrayed by the people who led to her incarceration and how she was angry with herself for making poor choices. Her own friends had lied to her. People she trusted told her that everything would be okay when that was far from the case.

Owing to the support of friends and loved ones, I received multiple packages—a rare occurrence behind bars. When I was unable to collect them in my name, a friend graciously accepted the packages for me. During one such instance, as I unwrapped my holiday package with Myra, her candid question brought into sharp focus the disparity between the worlds within and beyond prison walls.

Myra's query pierced through the celebration in the face of abundance: "What were your Christmas' like?" Her revelation left an indelible mark as I recounted cherished memories of warmth, family, and joy—she had never experienced Christmas. She had never had a real one as her parents immigrated to this country and did not have the resources to celebrate. I grew up poor too; I knew we didn't always get everything we asked for, and that a pot of beans and tortillas went a long way in our family. However, my parents always made sure our holidays were incredibly memorable. At that moment, the stark reality of privilege within the prison system became glaringly evident.

My family and friends ensured that I had money on my books, which gave me the luxury of being able to buy things I desired in the canteen. My friends could afford it, were willing to skirt the rules, and able to send additional packages for me (in other individuals' names) so I could have the things I liked. Most folks I was incarcerated with did not have this luxury. Most people in my hallway were unable to shop beyond what they made at their jobs.

Imagine being paid 18 cents an hour and living off of that. Or working in the kitchen knowing your family couldn't afford to buy you comfortable shoes, which a doctor noted as a medical need, that you had no other option but to steal food and sneak it back for a happier buyer in the yard. By living, I mean being able to buy basic needs like soap, shampoo, deodorant, and tooth-paste. The state did give indigent individuals the above items, but they weren't brands we were familiar with, and most com-plained of their efficacy.

Choosing to embrace C-over-C (a classification that lowered my privilege status) didn't bother me; it became my sanctuary, a res-pite from the monotony of daily struggles and the slave labor I had endured. The cold outside, the endless lines, and the indig-nities suffered at the hands of correctional officers led me to opt for a semblance of reprieve. No more unnecessary pat-downs that always brushed up against my private area. This decision, however, came at the cost of relinquishing certain privileges.

Mine came after I was exhausted from the labor-intensive roles I was given as a punishment for what I felt was just being me. I was no longer willing to work for free doing something that did not match my skill sets. It took me several years of institutionalization to speak up, but when I did, my world opened up to roommates and community members I would not usually bond with. I was exhausted from all of it. The harassment. The constant over-touching by officers during pat-downs. And let's not get started on the other women. I was physically, emotionally, and mentally exhausted.

Just a Shy Girl's Pain: A Mirror to Systemic Injustices

In the shadows of the C-over-C room, Myra's pain became emblematic of the systemic injustices woven into the carceral fabric. One night, I heard a muffled sound after everyone was fast asleep. Investigating further, I witnessed Myra physically release her anguish on the bathroom walls—an act that epitomized the desperation and anger entrenched within those condemned by a system that failed to deliver justice. I didn't make a big deal about what was happening as I would've possibly woken up everyone in the room. I also feared that a corrections officer might see her bruised and battered fists and assume the worst.

Worst here refers to the assumption that she was in a fight with a fellow prisoner. Alternately, it could potentially prompt the staff to toss our room and disturb our peace while taking contraband. As for me, I just felt sad for my friend. She had experienced too much hardship in her young life. The incarceration also separated her from her family and did not allow her to have a relationship with her child—a child who would never know her mom; a child raised by her grandparents in the same neighborhood that had all but destroyed Myra, an incredibly shy person. I knew it took a lot for her to share this pain with me and to trust me with her truth.

Addiction, a common thread in many incarcerated narratives, manifests differently within and beyond the prison walls. The pain, however, is universal. While I grappled with the challenges of institutionalized oppression, my journey took place in a more forgiving environment. The juxtaposition underscores the systemic failures inherent in the criminal justice system.

While I represent the complexities of institutionalization and the intersectionality of privilege within the prison ecosystem, Myra's plight is a poignant reminder that systemic issues extend beyond the visible bars. She was set up to fail. She was only seen as a bad girl undeserving of any type of investment—unworthy of anyone taking the time out to explain to this youngster what she was facing.

Our conversations unveil a shared commitment to understanding the multifaceted layers of incarceration. Healing, we acknowledge, requires dismantling the very structures that perpetuate harm. It is a collective call to address systemic flaws, fostering a society where compassion, justice, and rehabilitation triumph over the punitive nature of the current criminal justice paradigm.

As I delve deeper into my reflections on the disparities of privilege within the prison system, I'm compelled to explore the broader systemic flaws that perpetuate inequality and hinder the potential for genuine rehabilitation.

The prison yard, though a microcosm of societal issues, reflects a deeply entrenched bias that often determines the trajectory of individuals within the criminal justice system. Myra's story, marked by a grave clerical error and a misguided sense of trust in her gang, speaks volumes about the flawed mechanisms of the justice system. While she had been sentenced to two concurrent sentences, the courts noted it as consecutive, which caused more harm during her initial years inside of prison as she navigated correcting the legal error herself.

Moreover, the classification system, which labeled me as a high-security offender, sheds light on the subjective nature of judgments that significantly impact an individual's prison experience. How many others, like Myra and me, have fallen victim to administrative errors that alter the course of their incarceration?

The toll of incarceration on mental health is an unspoken reality that permeates every corner of the prison yard. Myra's tearful episode in the bathroom, stemming from the weight of her life sentence, unveils the inadequacy of mental health resources within these institutions. The institutional response to her emotional outburst exemplifies the dehumanizing aspects of the system, focusing more on potential disturbances than on the well-being of the incarcerated.

The institution did wrong by virtually everyone I encountered, including Myra, the shyest girl I have ever met. Had anyone taken the time to support and understand her struggle, she might be on her way home or already free today. She was a smart and talented young woman when I met her. She had a lot of hopes and dreams far beyond these walls; by not investing in her mental health, the system failed her.

Limited Privilege

Privilege, or the lack thereof, becomes a defining factor in accessing mental health support. I had a family I could call and who would advocate for me beyond the walls, and my relationships with the staff afforded me some respite as well. However, the majority faced the harsh reality of navigating their mental health struggles without adequate resources.

While I navigated the challenges of prison life, my experiences with Myra and others highlighted the importance of acknowledging the systemic injustices that exacerbate the hardships faced by incarcerated individuals. As I grappled with the emotional toll of witnessing fellow prisoners battle addiction and despair, the call for transformative justice echoed louder.

Our conversations within the confines of the C-over-C room were not merely exchanges of personal narratives; they became a rallying cry for justice reform. The prison yard, filled with stories of pain, resilience, and systemic failures, necessitates a comprehensive examination of policies and practices perpetuating harm cycles.

The complexities of privilege, as evidenced by the stark disparities within the prison system, underscore the urgency for a paradigm shift in our approach to justice. It calls for a model that prioritizes rehabilitation over punishment, addresses systemic biases, and recognizes the inherent humanity of every incarcerated individual.

In my ongoing journey, I advocate for a justice system that promotes healing and addresses the root causes of criminal behavior. Myra's story, intertwined with countless others, serves as a testament to the resilience of the human spirit, even in the face of institutional oppression.

As this exploration of the California prison yard in the 1990s unfolds, the power of connection emerges as a catalyst for change. The complexities of privilege, mental health struggles, and systemic flaws within the criminal justice system demand our collective attention.

In Myra's tearful moment and in my journey beyond privilege, there lies an unspoken call for transformative justice—a vision where stories become instruments of change, dismantling the oppressive structures that perpetuate cycles of suffering.

This discourse transcends the prison yard, inviting you to engage with the broader conversation on justice reform. It beckons all of us to confront uncomfortable truths and challenge ingrained biases. People are not defined by their ; they are not only worthy of redemption but in need of it.

7
Reclaiming Agency: Unlearning What No Longer Serves

Learning Objectives

1. Analyze the impact of the Three Strikes law on marginalized communities.
2. Explore intersectionality and solidarity within the prison environment.
3. Reflect on personal biases and commit to transformative justice.

Imprisonment became more than confinement; it was stacked with revelation—a space where injustices seeped through every crack in the system. If you looked into the eyes of enough prisoners, you would easily fall in. The hollow emptiness one often finds in the eyes of another was always apparent when I encountered someone who had lost hope. Hope for themselves. Hope for a world where justice would prevail. Hope for a future not promised.

As I shared quarters with seven roommates, predominantly mothers trapped in cycles of poverty and substance use, the disparities of our situations became glaringly apparent. The sadness was often infectious as was the hopelessness if you allowed it to. I could not blame a mother for her despair: not knowing what the future held; not knowing whether she would ever see her children; not knowing whether she would be able to feel whole again. I did fall into someone's darkness, but thankfully it was short lived as I read the book *Co-dependent No More* during that same time and allowed myself to have compassion for all those involved while keeping my hopes up. I had the privilege of meeting the author later in my life.

In the late 1990s and early 2000s, the criminal justice system was rife with injustices, particularly with the implementation of the Three Strikes law. Statistics from the ACLU revealed that California, where I found myself incarcerated, was among the states wielding this punitive measure most aggressively. The Golden State was far from golden. The law disproportionately affected marginalized communities, with Black and Latino individuals receiving harsher sentences for nonviolent offenses compared to our white counterparts.

Pops, a fellow prisoner and confidante, epitomized the systemic failures that defined my incarceration experiences. Serving a three-strike sentence for what amounted to minor infractions, Pops embodied the collateral damage of a system built on punishment rather than rehabilitation. Her story echoed that of countless others who are victims of a justice system that prioritized incarceration over intervention.

She was doing life. I was also handed two strikes for the same offense—a strike per victim, seldom heard of today, but a care-free tactic of prosecutors during the 1990s and early 2000s. Both our sentences made us cautionary examples to the community. 'Don't get caught up, or we will throw the book at you and toss the key'—a phrase all too familiar to people who grew up in the hoods or barrios of California.

The Three Strikes Law

The late 1990s marked a period of heightened punitive measures within the American criminal justice system, exemplified by the implementation of the Three Strikes law. While ostensibly aimed at targeting repeat offenders, this legislation disproportionately affected Black and Brown communities, thereby exacerbating existing disparities in incarceration rates.

The Three Strikes law was enacted in various forms across multiple states. The Three Strikes law mandated harsh penalties for individuals convicted of three or more felonies, often regardless of the severity of the offenses. In theory, the law aimed to deter habitual criminals and enhance public safety. However, in practice, its implementation led to a staggering increase in the incarceration rates of Black and Brown individuals, perpetuating cycles of systemic inequality and long-lasting social disenfranchisement.

One of the most glaring consequences of the Three Strikes law was its disproportionate impact on communities of color. According to research conducted by the ACLU and other advocacy organizations, Black and Latino individuals were significantly more likely to receive harsh sentences under this legislation compared to their white counterparts. The application of the law reflected deeply ingrained racial biases within the criminal justice system, perpetuating a cycle of discrimination and marginalization.

The punitive nature of the Three Strikes law increased the existing disparities in sentencing, particularly for nonviolent offenses. Minor infractions that would typically result in probation or community service were transformed into life-altering sentences, tearing families apart and destabilizing communities. For many Black and Brown individuals, the Three Strikes law became a tool of systemic oppression, trapping them in a web of punitive measures that offered little hope for rehabilitation, redemption, or freedom.

Moreover, the implementation of the Three Strikes law resulted in overcrowding in prisons and stretched the already limited resources within the criminal justice system. Rather than addressing the root causes of crime, such as poverty, lack of access to education housing, and systemic racism, policymakers opted for punitive measures that perpetuated cycles of incarceration and recidivism.

In the context of my own experiences behind bars, the impacts of the Three Strikes law were palpable. Many of my fellow prisoners, including Pops, found themselves ensnared in a punitive system that offered little room for redemption or rehabilitation. Their stories echoed those of countless others—victims of a justice system that prioritized punishment over compassion, retribution over restoration.

Intersectionality in Community

As we grappled with the realities of incarceration, it became increasingly clear that the Three Strikes law was not merely a reflection of societal attitudes toward crime but a manifestation of systemic racism and inequality. The institution and its staff seemed to hate us for our resilience. Its legacy continues to reverberate through generations of Black and Brown communities, serving as a stark reminder of the enduring legacy of racial injustice within the American criminal justice system.

In the confines of our shared space, Pops and I engaged in late-night conversations that laid bare the realities of institutionalized racism and systemic oppression. We dissected the intersecting layers of privilege, examining our roles in perpetuating systems of injustice. For me, an LGBTQ Latinx crime survivor with proximity to whiteness who experienced generational poverty, and for Pops, a Black butch dyke from Venice Beach, our identities were both shields (depending on where we were) and shackles in the face of adversity.

Our discussions unearthed uncomfortable truths about the racism endemic within ourselves and the institution. From discriminatory policies to microaggressions in everyday interactions, the prison environment mirrored the injustices entrenched in society at large. Pops and I navigated this maze of oppression with a shared commitment to authenticity, refusing to compromise our identities in the face of it all.

Yet, even within the confines of our shared space, divisions persisted. In a system designed to pit prisoners against each other, solidarity became a revolutionary act—a defiance of the status quo. As a queer individual, I found myself straddling multiple identities, each fraught with its own set of challenges. But I discovered the true essence of liberation in the solidarity of shared struggle. Pops was my chosen family, as were so many others.

Our experiences behind bars were not anomalies but symptomatic of broader societal injustices. According to the Sentencing Project, the rate of incarceration of Black Americans is five times higher than that of white Americans, with Latino individuals also disproportionately represented in the criminal justice system. These disparities reflect systemic inequalities that permeate every facet of our society, from housing and employment to education and healthcare.

In honoring Pops' legacy, may she rest in peace, I recommit myself to the fight for justice, equity, and liberation. Our bond transcended the confines of prison walls, a testament to the transformative power of solidarity in the face of adversity. As I continue my journey beyond incarceration, her spirit remains a guiding light, illuminating the path toward a more just and equitable future.

I challenge all of you to honor Pops by having intersectional conversations with somebody who shares some but perhaps not all of your identities. Dig deep into those relationships that challenge you to think outside your needs, wants, and desires and explore those of others with unique perspectives. One often finds themselves surprised at how alike we are as humans; our differences are often places of learning for all.

8
Maintaining Sanity in the "Free World"

Learning Objectives

1. Explore reintegration challenges faced by former prisoners.
2. Examine the concept of sanity and resilience post-incarceration.
3. Discuss abolitionist praxis as a framework for social justice activism.

The term "free world" first resonated with me in the confines of a cramped cell, as I was surrounded by the restless energy of incarcerated women yearning for liberation. As I dreamed of stepping into the now elusive realm of freedom, I grappled with the challenge of keeping my sanity within the walls of confinement.

Navigating the winding corridors of incarceration demanded resilience and resolve. Amid the discord of loud sounds and bustling energies, I learned to cultivate a sense of inner peace—a sanctuary forged through therapy, community support, and a commitment to abolitionist principles. My journey toward wholeness became a testament to the transformative power of solidarity and resistance.

The term "free world" is often used by prisoners to describe life outside prison. This terminology reflects the stark contrast between the constraints of incarceration and the perceived freedom of the outside world. For individuals who have been incarcerated, the notion of "free world" represents a realm of possibilities, autonomy, and liberation that is often denied within the confines of prison walls.

Psychologically, the "free world" concept can have profound implications for individuals transitioning from incarceration to society. For many former prisoners, reentering the "free world" is challenging and uncertain. While the prospect of freedom may initially evoke hope and anticipation, it can also trigger anxiety, apprehension, and a sense of disorientation.

I understand this all too well. The day I was released from prison tested every fiber of my being: from being an immediate release due to clerical error to being forced to wait hours after everyone's release that day for the warden's signature with little to no communication to my family—who were eagerly waiting for me—to finding my dress-out package mysteriously missing. They found the package almost a month later and charged me to send it home. It was the insult to injury that stung. I knew my family had put this box together with explicit instructions on how I wanted to meet freedom.

Our first stop was a shoe store, where all the choices overwhelmed me. At one point, I exited the shoe store and hyperventilated as this was the first time I was allowed to pick what I want in almost seven years, and there were just too many choices. I went from being told what I could and couldn't have to having a wall filled with size 9 men's shoes to choose from. I eventually made my selection, as the shower shoe I was wearing didn't make me feel like I was free.

Navigating the Not-so-Free World

Transitioning from prison to the "free world" entails navigating a complex web of social, economic, and emotional barriers. Many individuals face formidable obstacles, including limited access to housing, employment, education, healthcare, and social support networks. The stigma of incarceration, coupled with systemic barriers and discrimination, can exacerbate feelings of margin- alization and alienation, further complicating the process of reintegration.

What's more, the pressure to conform to societal expectations and norms in the "free world" can be overwhelming for individ- uals grappling with the trauma and stigma of incarceration. The fear of relapse or recidivism looms large, as returning to prison represents not only a loss of freedom but also a rupture in one's sense of self and identity.

For some individuals, the allure of the "free world" may be overshadowed by the challenges of readjustment and the temptations of familiar patterns and environments. The risk of reoffending, whether due to limited opportunities, lack of sup- port, or unresolved trauma, underscores the urgent need for comprehensive reentry services and support systems.

Ultimately, the transition from prison to the "free world" is a complex and multifaceted process that requires empathy, understanding, and a commitment to addressing the structural inequities and systemic injustices that perpetuate cycles of incarceration and recidivism for each individual. By recognizing the inherent dignity and humanity of individuals impacted by the criminal justice system, we can work toward creating a more inclusive and equitable society where everyone has the chance to thrive and contribute to the collective well-being.

The Pursuit of Sanity

Rooted in abolition, my pursuit of sanity transcended personal healing to encompass a broader vision of collective liberation. It was an acknowledgment of the interdependence of our struggles—a recognition that none of us could truly be free until all of us were free. As I bore witness to the insidious manifestations of white supremacy and systemic oppression, I vowed to stand in solidarity with marginalized communities, particularly my Black, trans, and nonbinary siblings, whose struggles stand for the urgency of our collective resistance.

Dreaming, once a source of torment and anguish, became an act of defiance—a refusal to surrender to the limitations imposed by society. In the aftermath of incarceration, plagued by nightmares and post-traumatic stress, the act of dreaming became a radical assertion of agency—a refusal to be defined by past traumas and present circumstances. It was a testament to the resilience of the human spirit—a refusal to succumb to the despair that threatened to engulf us.

Maintaining sanity in a world marred by injustice and inequality became an act of resistance—a commitment to living out our values in the face of adversity. It required constant vigilance against the corrosive forces of anger and despair as well as a willingness to confront the systemic injustices that threatened to erode our humanity. It was a recognition that every individual, regardless of their past actions or circumstances, possessed inherent worth and dignity—a belief at the heart of abolitionist praxis.

Embracing Abolition

Abolition, for me, was not merely a theoretical framework but a lived practice—a commitment to dismantling the structures of oppression that perpetuated cycles of violence and harm. It was a recognition of the interconnectedness of our struggles—a rejection of the punitive logic underpinning the carceral state. Through abolitionist practices, I sought to confront the root causes of over-incarceration and systemic violence, advocating for community-based alternatives rooted in principles of justice and equity.

In embracing abolition, I found solace amid the chaos—a sense of purpose and meaning transcending confinement's boundaries. It was a recognition that true sanity lay not in conformity to oppressive norms but in pursuing justice and liberation for all. It was a commitment to challenging the status quo and dismantling the systems of oppression that sought to devalue and dehumanize our communities.

As I navigate the complexities of the free world, I remain steadfast in my commitment to abolitionist principles. It is a journey filled with challenges and setbacks yet fueled by a profound sense of hope and possibility. In the face of adversity, I draw strength from the resilience of those who have come before me—the count-less voices of resistance and courage that continue to inspire and empower me.

The easiest of all these practices has been community care and support. You can regularly find me giving back to my commu-nity in ways outside of the organization I run. As an abolitionist, I believe in fostering community care and support as an alterna-tive to punitive measures in every way possible. It is evident in my work as a leader and the ongoing ideas planted in the young adults I work with. I impress others to gain an understanding that addressing the root causes of crime and harm requires building strong social networks and providing resources to those in need.

I have gained a new appreciation of restorative justice practices in all things I do. As part of my commitment to restorative justice, I have initiated opportunities to address conflicts and grievances including issues within my leadership. Instead of getting defen-sive, I have encouraged colleagues to engage in open communi-cation and empathetic listening to resolve issues collaboratively. Through these circles, we promote accountability, healing, and mutual understanding among coworkers.

9
Walking into Wholeness

Learning Objectives

1. Understand the challenges and opportunities faced by individuals navigating life after conviction.
2. Examine community empowerment and social justice activism.
3. Introduce abolition as a movement to dismantle oppressive systems.

As I walked the institution's halls, correctional officers often called me an "inmate," a label that never quite fit. In my eyes, I was a prisoner, held against my will, navigating a system that I had not chosen nor did I understand and was forced to be a part of. Despite accepting my sentence through a plea bargain, I refused to internalize the dehumanizing language that sought to diminish my humanity. Had anyone shared the harsh realities and untold truths of taking a deal, I might have relented and fought back. Make no mistake, although I was guilty, I did not have shame about my crime. I was not proud of my behavior, but I did know I deserved respect.

Without fail, every time I left my room or cell, I had some over-paid babysitter aka a correctional officer yell at me for one thing or another. For example, one time I was criticized for my pants being too baggy; it was not my fault that I was losing weight because it was the institution that had me working on yard crew. Work involved what felt like mowing several football fields with a push mower. Another instance was being questioned regularly about whether I had a chrono[1] for those "free-world" shoes I was wearing. In fact, I did have a chrono from a medical professional stating my need for shoes that offered me some actual support. The truth was that I advocated tirelessly to secure each of the chronos I obtained.

Chronos

Prison institution chronos are official records that are part of a prisoners central file and can have a substantial impact on various aspects of their prison life, including classification, eligibility for parole, and access to privileges.

General Chrono (Form 128-G): This is used for documenting general information about any prisoner that is important but not directly related to disciplinary actions. Examples include participation in educational programs, vocational training, or counseling sessions, as well as interactions with staff that are noteworthy but not necessarily negative.

Disciplinary Chrono (Form 128-A): This form is used to document minor disciplinary infractions that do not warrant a formal Rules Violation Report (RVR). It might include incidents like minor rule violations, failure to follow instructions, or other behaviors that, while not severe, still need to be documented for the prisoner's record.

Medical/Mental Health Chrono (Form 128-MH): These chronos are used to record information related to a prisoner's health, including medical treatments, mental health evaluations, and any observations relevant to the prisoner's physical or mental well-being.

Confidential Chrono: Some chronos contain sensitive or confidential information, such as details related to gang affiliations, informant status, or other security concerns. These are kept separate from the general file to protect the safety and security of both the prisoner and the institution.

Chronos are typically completed by prison staff, including correctional officers, counselors, medical professionals, or other personnel who have direct interactions with the prisoner. Once completed, they are added to the prisoner's central file, which is maintained by the institution.

Chronos play a crucial role in the decision-making process regarding a prisoner's classification level, housing assignments, eligibility for parole, and participation in various prison programs. For instance, a series of positive chronos might support a prisoner's request for reduced custody status or participation in rehabilitative programs. Conversely, negative chronos, especially those documenting repeated rule violations or poor behavior, could result in disciplinary actions, loss of privileges, or a higher security classification.

Chronos are reviewed during parole hearings and other evaluations to assess a prisoner's behavior and rehabilitation progress. Parole boards may consider the content of chronos when deciding whether to grant parole, thus making these documents influential in determining a prisoner's release.

Prison institution chronos serve as a comprehensive record of a prisoner's time in prison, documenting their behavior, interactions, and progress. They are critical tools for prison administration to monitor prisoners, guide decision-making, and ensure that the institutional record reflects the individual's conduct and rehabilitation efforts

My favorite was being told to put my hair up or watch my smart mouth. I was in my early twenties and ready to engage in every type of debate. I had just resolved that the staff were miserable, and their life sentence outweighed mine. In those moments of resistance, seeds of discontent were planted, sparking a desire for something better. As my release date approached, bureaucratic errors prolonged my incarceration, underscoring the arbitrary nature of the system. Yet, amid the frustration and injustice, I found solace in the community I had forged behind bars.

When I say error, I mean that someone who worked in an administrative role in the records dept literally misread the judge's minute order. While I was sentenced to six years and two strikes for my controlling case, I also had two other nonviolent charges which were both charged at eight months to be served concurrent to one another and consecutive to my controlling case. That means I was sentenced to six years and eight months but this administrator read it as seven years and four months.

If I hadn't had the agency to call upon my counselor and point out the error and prove it with documentation, they would have kept me for as long as they could have. While one might consider this false imprisonment, it is not that easy to prove or to be reimbursed for the error. I just wanted to be free. Later, upon release, I would forgo suing them for keeping me longer than sentenced to have a shorter parole period.

To say I hated all correction officers would be a lie. I disliked many of them and hated a small handful. I respected those who treated me with the dignity and respect I deserved. There were only but a few but they still existed, and for this, I am thankful for them. They reminded me of my humanity and that everyone deserves to be treated with dignity and respect. It was simple things like asking me versus demanding I pick up something they dropped. Or asking me, and I mean with genuine concern, as to how I was doing or feeling.

One example I recall is when I was doing time during the terrorist attacks on 9/11. I was the only prisoner out doing my laundry early in the morning and while me and Mr. Brown[2] sat on two different couches, we were both watching *Good Morning America* as the towers went down. He checked on me every day that week to ensure I was okay and also shared details about the incident. Mr. Brown cared and understood how important it was to treat someone with dignity. He would often remind me that I was more than my worst mistake and worthy of redemption.

The connections I formed with fellow prisoners, individuals who had challenged and seen me for who I was, provided a sense of perspective and belonging. We didn't care about what each of us was serving time for(unless you hurt a child) and reserved judgment. Together, we confronted the harsh realities of incarceration, grappling with the systemic injustices that had brought us together. Thankfully, the community sowed the seeds of transformation within this gauntlet of adversity. Thank goodness or my story could've been a lot different there: I could have given up on myself; I could've given up on all of us.

Whenever my mom visited me, she would always say she prayed that my heart would never harden. She prayed that I would remain that person who would use my heart to touch another's. That compassion would always remain a part of my ethos. Her prayers worked. My prayers worked as I walked into wholeness and loved myself despite my situation. I was way more than the sum of my worst mistakes, as were the other folks I shared the yard with. We live in a world where so many people have been criminalized out of fear with policies that disproportionately impact those of us who come from over-policed communities.

While I rejected the arbitrariness and, often, pettiness of the institution, I was more than rehabilitated. I was finding my way back to my wholeness. That was my goal. I was preparing my mind and heart to be everything that everyone had dreamed of for me—the person I knew I was meant to be—and I loved myself through all the hard times.

Wholeness refers to a state of completeness, integration, and authenticity within oneself. It encompasses emotional, psychological, and spiritual well-being, achieved through self-awareness, self-acceptance, and self-care. Walking into wholeness involves confronting past traumas and reclaiming agency over one's life and identity. It is a journey of self-discovery and self-empowerment characterized by resilience, growth, and transformation. In the context of one's narrative, wholeness represents a process of healing and redemption, where you navigate the complexities of your lived experiences to find a deeper sense of peace and purpose. While this process wasn't for everyone, I dove in. From self-help classes to jailhouse pedicures. Whatever it took.

Now when I say whatever it took, I do not mean the same solutions that I had prior to incarceration. It meant I would have to work within legal structures and give up the allure of fast, easy money. It meant I would have to face the world's rejection as a person with a record and handle the collateral consequences that came with it, learning to shake it off. While I was not familiar with how this would look like based on the conversations with reoccurring offenders, I knew I was going to have to be the me I was born to be.

Life Outside

Upon my release in January of 2004, I navigated the unfamiliar terrain of freedom with trepidation, aware of the privilege and opportunities that lay before me. As I ventured into the world beyond prison walls, I confronted my fears and insecurities, reclaiming agency over my life and identity as I stumbled through new experiences. And when I say stumbled, I mean stumbled. Take for example my first anxiety attack at the shoe store. Too many choices had me taking deep cleansing breaths outside before I could be met with the multitude of choices I now had in comparison with having to make my selection based on a picture sent in my quarterly package. Now I own far too many shoes and have to remind myself to alternate.

At the time in California, individuals with a criminal record faced numerous post-conviction restrictions that significantly impacted their lives. These include barriers to employment, housing, voting, and access to certain public benefits. Many jobs in California required background checks, and individuals with convictions, particularly felonies, may be disqualified from certain professions, especially those requiring state licensing (e.g., healthcare, teaching, and law enforcement). Even where legally permissible, employers often use criminal records to reject applicants. These laws have improved ever so slightly.

Certain convictions can render an individual ineligible for public assistance programs like food stamps (CalFresh) and housing assistance. With over half of the population entering prison at or below the poverty level and having relied heavily on these resources for basic survival, they return with access to nothing upon their release. Could you imagine being given a mere $200 when released from prison and told that this is all you get to try and make it outside? I relished when I passed "go" and got that $200 in Monopoly money until this became a reality. While I had the support of my family and friends, most did not, and these resources were often gone within days, leaving a person helpless and desperate with the threats of being reincarcerated hanging over their heads.

Individuals with criminal records often face discrimination in the housing market. Many landlords conduct background checks and reject applications from those with convictions. Public housing programs also have restrictions that exclude individuals with specific criminal histories. If you find a landlord who will look past that, the offer will come with strings attached, all of which mean poor living conditions. Recently, one of my colleagues went on to get his master's degree not because he was excited about education but because his family needed housing. Could you imagine being forced into additional educational debt so that you and your growing family could have safety?

While California has made strides in restoring voting rights to individuals on parole, those currently incarcerated for a felony conviction remain disenfranchised. Despite significant efforts to register and support those in jail who are yet to be convicted to exercise their voting rights, it is often met with additional obstacles varying by the county, law enforcement agency, and head jailer. Thus, rights aren't always attainable, not just because of the people involved, but also depending on who's in charge.

Across the United States, post-conviction restrictions vary widely by state but generally include employment, housing, voting, public assistance restrictions, and professional licensing. Some states have "ban the box" laws that prevent employers from asking about criminal history on initial job applications, but these laws are not universal. Voting rights for individuals with felony convictions also vary by state. Some states, like Maine and Vermont, allow incarcerated individuals to vote, while others impose lifetime disenfranchisement for certain offenses. Nationally, individuals with criminal records often face barriers to private housing and public assistance, with federal housing policies imposing strict eligibility criteria. Many states restrict individuals with criminal records from obtaining professional licenses, which can block access to well-paying jobs in a range of fields, from cosmetology to law. Ironically, it was a cosmetology was vocation offered inside women's prisons during my incarceration.

These post-conviction restrictions create significant obstacles for individuals trying to reintegrate into society after serving their sentences. The inability to secure stable employment or housing, coupled with the loss of voting rights and access to public benefits, perpetuates cycles of poverty and recidivism. This marginalization disproportionately affects communities of color, exacerbating existing inequalities.

Numerous organizations at both the state and national levels are advocating for reforms to reduce these barriers. These organizations are driving legislative and policy changes aimed at dismantling post-conviction barriers, promoting restorative justice, and creating opportunities for individuals to rebuild their lives after incarceration. Thankfully, I had the chance in 2022 to do just that by being employed by Alliance for Safety and Justice's Timedone program, where we helped pass the most progressive post-conviction relief in the nation. In the world. It created a pathway for almost anyone who went to prison to petition the court to have it expunged. I was going to be free! I had helped tens of thousands overcome this barrier, and I was confident I'd be able to do it for myself too.

For me, walking into wholeness meant confronting the trauma of incarceration and reclaiming my humanity in the process. It meant embracing vulnerability and resilience, acknowledging the wounds of the past while charting a path toward healing, forgiveness, and societal redemption. While I was still going to be a radical and speak my mind, I had a new role as an active listener for my community.

In 2006, one of the pivotal moments in my journey toward wholeness came through my involvement with Getting Out by Going In (GOGI), an organization dedicated to empowering incarcerated individuals through cognitive skill-building and personal development. Volunteering with this organization allowed me to witness the transformative power of community and solidarity, instilling a sense of purpose and direction within me. As I immersed myself in advocacy and community organizing, I witnessed firsthand the profound impact of systemic oppression on marginalized communities. The injustices that had once confined me behind bars now fueled my determination to effect change and challenge the status quo. This was not how things should be constantly popping into my head.

When I was released from incarceration, the world outside felt familiar yet alien. I was free, but the weight of my conviction clung to me like a shadow. My first major decision was to decline participation in a program in Watts, which would shape my path unexpectedly. I didn't want to live in the hood anymore. I know it sounds elitist, and I struggle with being honest about it. However, as a non-Black person of color who passes for white on most days, I was exhausted from fighting with other Latine people. I just wanted to move forward with my life away from neighborhoods that I had caused harm in.

Instead of attending a structured program, I moved into a sober living as there were very few choices available in the area I wanted to live in. I also easily found employment in the entertainment industry, where creativity and hard work often overshadowed one's past. I found a niche as a scenic, working behind the scenes to create the visual magic that brings stories to life. This job wasn't just a means of survival but an arena where I could express myself and rebuild my identity. I loved everything about the space, from the smell of paint to wood being sanded. I got to work on shows like *Big Brother* setting up their "cloud room" one season and hanging out in the back yard setting up the space. There were other shows as well but working on *Big Brother* was a unique experience.

During this period, love found its way into my life. I met my partner, and we shared an immediate and profound connection. We both just wanted to be accepted in a world that did not seem to want us. From friendship to understanding, we have seen and done it all in the last 19 years of being together. We saved each other and have built this incredible life today. When I say incredible, I often times have to pinch myself. We own a home, with a smaller house in the back for my aging mother, have several late model cars, and have traveled across the globe—Okay, to countries that will allow my visit! We still dream of visiting the United Kingdom as my wife's ancestors are from there. One day!

Who would have thought that seizing the brief window to marry during the Prop 8 era, an act of defiance and hope, would bring us all we have today. The joy of our union was soon overshadowed by the more significant battle for marriage equality, Prop 8. Our love story became a cornerstone of my activism, fueling my passion to fight for the rights of all LGBTQ individuals. I attended the church in Fresno, California, that organized Prop 8, and thus the fight was extra personal to me.

It was during this time that I realized the power of personal narratives. It opened doors for me to share my story and teach others how to share theirs. I saw firsthand how storytelling could break down prejudices and build bridges of understanding and solidarity. This advocacy work became my mission, intertwining with my journey toward equality and fairness. While I was out of the closet on all accounts, I shied away from talking about incarceration as it was still raw and I was healing.

My entrepreneurial spirit led me to the cannabis industry during the Prop 215 era (1996–2016), where I pioneered the first statewide cannabis delivery service. Navigating the legal landscape as someone with a record was daunting. The legal implications were significant, but I was determined to discover a legitimate space in this emerging market. This venture gave me a livelihood and underscored the broader fight for cannabis legalization and criminal justice reform.

When I say legal implications, I mean I was ostensibly at risk of being reincarcerated. However, if you shared space with the families I worked with, and if you heard not only their gratitude but their pain and anguish over the suffering of their loved one, you would understand. I witnessed firsthand how family dynamics changed for the better when the family member who was ill had access to cannabis, and I was just grateful to play a small little role. This was how I honored my queer friends who died during the AIDS crisis. While I struggled to believe cannabis was medicine in the 1990s, I deepened my understanding through these families.

One of my most significant contributions to social justice was helping to launch National Expungement Week. Under my leadership, this initiative gained momentum, providing critical legal relief to thousands of individuals burdened by their criminal records. The success stories from these events were numerous and deeply gratifying, each a testament to the power of collective action and resilient leadership—from inspiring and training other leaders across the country to sharing strategies and just doing the work.

Throughout my journey, I have learned that freedom is not merely the absence of incarceration but the presence of opportunity, equality, and the right to be heard. By sharing my story and empowering others to share theirs, I continue to fight for a world where justice and love prevail.

This led me to begin exploring the writings and thoughts of leaders who had similarly faced or studied incarceration and oppression. From Dr. Martin Luther King's letters while incarcerated to the incomparable Angela Davis to Ruth Wilson Gilmore, I was committing my life to figuring it out. There was backlash from some community members as I explored ideas of abolition and readily shared my views on the topic. Yet, what followed reminded me of the enduring legacy of white supremacy and discrimination. In the face of adversity, I resolved to channel my energy into community-building and resistance, seeking to create spaces of belonging and affirmation for all.

Introduction to Abolition

As a politicized person, the abolitionist movement to dismantle systems of oppression and develop alternatives rooted in justice, equity, and liberation resonated with my soul. When I learned that it encompasses various forms of activism and advocacy aimed at challenging and transforming oppressive institutions, including the criminal justice system, prisons, and policing, I was beyond in. Finally, I found a word that described my dreams. Since abolition seeks to address the root causes of social injustice, including racism, poverty, and inequality, by reimagining governance and community care systems, I believed, if not me, then who?

Central to my belief in the inherent dignity and worth of every individual, as well as the recognition of systemic violence and harm perpetuated by punitive approaches to social problems, it was an easy fit. In our narratives, abolition represents a commitment to challenging the status quo, advocating for systemic change, and building communities rooted in principles of solidarity, mutual aid, and collective liberation.

Abolition Is...	Abolition Isn't...
A movement to dismantle systems of oppression	A call for chaos or lawlessness
	An endorsement of harm or violence
Rooted in transformative justice and social change	Merely the absence of prisons or police
Advocating for alternatives to punishment and incarceration	A single-issue movement focused solely on the criminal justice system
	A utopian vision devoid of practicality
Centered on community empowerment and healing	An individualistic approach to justice

Post-Incarceration to Present Day

Through initiatives like the National Expungement Week, I endeavored to dismantle the barriers that perpetuated cycles of incarceration and disenfranchisement. It was a journey filled with challenges and setbacks, fueled by a steadfast commitment to justice and liberation.

In my quest for wholeness, I found solace in community and connection, in the shared struggle for dignity and equality. Through introspection and self-discovery, I unearthed the seeds of abolition within myself, recognizing the inherent power and agency that resided within each of us.

As I continue to walk this path of healing and transformation, I am guided by the belief that all individuals possess the capacity for redemption and renewal. It is through collective action and solidarity that we can usher in a future defined by justice, equity, and compassion.

Exploring the themes of wholeness and abolition in one's narrative offers folks a deeper understanding of the transformative power of resilience, community, and social justice activism. These concepts serve as guiding principles in our journey toward healing, empowerment, and social change.

I led Los Angeles' cannabis social equity movement in 2017, securing $9 million from the city council to fund and establish a social equity program. Realizing the need for more and with community direction, the Social Impact Center (TSIC) was born—a hub for organizers harmed by the War on Drugs and the war on the poor. A war that is far from being over.

The cannabis social equity movement is deeply intertwined with social justice, focusing on rectifying the historic injustices of the War on Drugs and the disproportionate harm inflicted on Black, Indigenous, People of Color (BIPOC), and marginalized communities. Beginning in the mid-twentieth century, the criminalization of cannabis was a key element in systemic racial discrimination, where drug laws were weaponized to target primarily Black and Latinx communities. The subsequent decades saw mass incarceration fueled by racially biased enforcement of drug laws, leaving generations of BIPOC individuals with criminal records, loss of economic opportunities, and fractured communities.

The modern cannabis social equity movement emerged as a response to this legacy of harm, particularly gaining traction in the 2010s alongside the growing wave of cannabis decriminalization and legalization. Advocates such as Dr. Amanda Reiman, who worked with a host of other players along the supply chain to develop the compassionate care model for medical cannabis in California, and organizations such as the Hood Incubator, TSIC (which I co-founded), and Cage-Free Repair (I sit on their board) have been instrumental in driving conversations about restorative justice, racial equity, and inclusion within the cannabis industry. Their advocacy has aimed to ensure that those most impacted by prohibition have access to the new economic opportunities within the legal cannabis market.

A key goal of the social equity movement is to create an industry that is diverse and inclusive and actively addresses the harms caused by decades of criminalization. This includes policies that prioritize the expungement of cannabis-related criminal records,

facilitate access to business licensing and capital for BIPOC entrepreneurs, and ensure the profits of cannabis legalization flow back
into affected communities. In Los Angeles and beyond, leaders
such as current councilwoman Eunisses Hernandez and policymakers such as California Senator Steven Bradford have pushed
for legislation that mandates these equity-focused frameworks.

However, despite these strides, equity in the cannabis industry
remains a challenge. Many social equity applicants face significant barriers to entry, including high license costs, limited access
to financing, and complex regulations. Predatory business practices and consolidation within the industry have further marginalized smaller, equity-focused businesses. While there are
some successes, for example, programs in cities like Oakland
and Los Angeles, the movement continues to struggle against
entrenched systems of inequality, requiring ongoing advocacy
and reform to fully realize a just and equitable cannabis economy.

Today, the cannabis social equity movement remains a crucial vehicle for broader social justice, intertwining economic
empowerment with the fight against racialized criminalization.
Through storytelling, policy advocacy, and coalition-building,
organizations and leaders within the movement are striving to
repair the damage done by the War on Drugs and create sustainable, stigma-free futures for BIPOC and LGBTQ+ communities. It
is also where the idea of building something that was inclusive
to all was born.

At TSIC, we build power in criminalized BIPOC and LGBTQ+ communities through stigma-free organizing and mutual aid. Our
model is rooted in storytelling, education, cultural expression,
intergenerational healing, and intersectional coalition building.

Our first program, expungement, a burdensome process insti-tuted by the very system that restricts the lives of formerly incarcerated people launched in 2018, has trained organizers nationwide and helped expunge records for tens of thousands. In 2021, collaborating with the DA's office, we identified and expunged records for 58k Angelinos.

In 2022, I helped pass California's SB731, opening doors for mil-lions to seek expungement. Through my expungement journey in 2023, with the help of lived experience, mental health, and legal experts, we developed our Leadership Through Service Program, which centers on trauma-informed training and com-munity collaboration.

10
Finding Redemption and Reward

Learning Objectives

1. Understand collateral consequences and their impact on individuals with criminal records.
2. Discuss the importance of expungement in promoting reintegration.
3. Embrace abolitionist principles for personal and collective transformation.

My journey as an organizer has been defined by resilience, advocacy, and community empowerment. As the co-founder and now executive director of TSIC, I have had the honor of influencing criminal justice reform, promoting social equity in cannabis legalization, and fighting for LGBTQ+ and BIPOC rights in Los Angeles and nationwide. My work spans various critical movements and campaigns, including GOGI, Prop 8, Courage Campaign, Prop 64, the Los Angeles Cannabis social equity movement, California's SB731, and expungement efforts nationwide. This final chapter reflects on my trajectory, highlighting the milestones and unwavering commitment that have shaped my path.

My reentry activism began with my involvement in GOGI, an organization dedicated to helping incarcerated individuals develop cognitive life skills for successful reintegration into society. This early work provided me with a foundational understanding of the systemic challenges faced by incarcerated individuals and the importance of comprehensive reentry support.

While only home for six months, I knew I had to find ways to be of service, and when I saw a volunteer opportunity with youth in Inglewood, CA, with an organization called GOGI, I jumped at the chance. I wanted them to hear it from someone with lived experience, and this experience ignited my passion for criminal justice reform.

In 2008, California's Proposition 8 aimed to ban same-sex marriage, sparking widespread controversy and mobilizing activists across the state. I joined the Courage Campaign, a progressive organization fighting against Prop 8. Through grassroots organizing, community outreach, and storytelling, I played a crucial role in advocating for marriage equality.

The battle against Prop 8 was a defining moment in my activism. It taught me the power of collective action and reinforced my commitment to LGBTQ+ rights.

The passage of Proposition 64 in 2016, which legalized recreational cannabis in California, marked a significant victory for the cannabis reform movement. However, I recognized the need to address the historical injustices faced by marginalized communities disproportionately affected by the War on Drugs. As a staunch advocate for social equity, I worked tirelessly to ensure that the benefits of cannabis legalization extended to BIPOC communities.

My efforts included advocating for social equity programs that prioritized licenses and resources for individuals from communities disproportionately impacted by drug criminalization. This work aimed to rectify past harms and create opportunities for economic empowerment within the cannabis industry.

The launch of the Black Lives Matter movement ignited a global reckoning with systemic racism, police brutality, and the deep historical wounds inflicted upon Black communities. For me, and many leaders like myself who are non-Black people of color, this moment of awakening brought a profound realization: we had a crucial role to play in ensuring that our Black siblings saw real healing and justice.

While I had long been committed to the fight for justice, the uprising in response to the murders of George Floyd, Breonna Taylor, and countless others illuminated the need for deeper solidarity. The fight for equity and justice could not be separated from the fight for Black liberation. We, as non-Black people of color, needed to confront the ways in which we had benefitted from systems of oppression and take active steps to dismantle them.

This awakening was not just about racial justice in the abstract— it was about tangible action. It was about ensuring that the cannabis industry, which had so often criminalized and disproportionately targeted Black communities, became a vehicle for healing and economic empowerment. Our Black siblings, who had endured generational trauma and had risked their freedom to provide access to cannabis, deserved to reap the benefits of this newly legalized industry.

Economic Opportunities and Ancestral Connection

Cannabis is not just a plant—it is a medicine, deeply rooted in the ancestral histories of many communities, particularly those from the Global South. For Black and Brown communities, cannabis has long been a source of healing and survival, even as it was criminalized by the state. Families had risked everything—from their freedom to their safety—to cultivate, distribute, and use this plant as a form of resistance and sustenance.

As cannabis legalization swept across California, it became clear that these communities, who had borne the brunt of the War on Drugs, deserved more than just recognition—they deserved a rightful share of the economic opportunities that came with legalization. TSIC has been at the forefront of this fight, advocating for policies that prioritize Black and Brown entrepreneurs and ensuring that the cannabis industry does not replicate the same inequities that plagued it under prohibition.

The economic empowerment of communities with an ancestral connection to cannabis is about more than financial gain—it's about healing. It's about restoring what was taken from us: our dignity, our freedom, our right to exist and thrive. Through our advocacy for social equity programs, we've sought to ensure that the individuals who risked their freedom to provide access to cannabis for their families are given the opportunity to participate in this once-in-a-lifetime industry. It is my dream to create a cooperative model that truly centers those of us impacted as worker members with ownership.

The Founding of the Social Impact Center

The Social Impact Center (TSIC) was born out of a desire to create healing for communities devastated by the War on Drugs, just as the cannabis industry, a once-in-a-lifetime opportunity, was emerging. Our founding was driven by a commitment to ensure that the benefits of legalization were not limited to corporations but extended to the communities most harmed by decades of criminalization. Most importantly, it was time that we started having conversations about the War on Drugs as a plural. It was time to show that —it was an attack on Black and Brown communities who, for generations, engaged in its consumption, distribution, and sought access. .

In 2019, after extensive organizing, advocacy, and community efforts, we successfully influenced the Los Angeles City Council to allocate $9 million toward funding the social equity program—a new initiative that's a part of their Department of Cannabis Regulation. This allocation directly resulted from grassroots efforts that I and other activists spearheaded. I even got to make a city council member cry and remember that "The fight is never about grapes or lettuce. It is always about people" (Cesar Chavez). Must've resonated. It marked a pivotal moment in our fight to ensure that those most impacted by drug policies had a seat at the table.

Around the same time, I was deeply involved in the creation and expansion of National Expungement Week, a nationwide effort to provide legal relief to those burdened by criminal records, particularly for cannabis-related convictions. Through our work with

National Expungement Week, we demonstrated the profound impact of clearing criminal records, thereby enabling individuals to access housing, employment, and other opportunities that had been previously denied to them. I taught people who had never organized in community how to do it. I built toolkits to support their efforts and mentored anyone who wanted to be a part of creating lasting change for people with convictions.

TSIC emerged from these dual efforts: advocating for social equity in cannabis and participating in expungement campaigns. Our mission remains rooted in stigma-free organizing, mutual aid, education, and storytelling. I continue to lead initiatives focused on providing comprehensive support to individuals from criminalized BIPOC and LGBTQ+ communities.

The center believes that the key problem that needs urgent solutions is systemic criminalization. Rooted in white supremacy, gendered violence, and racial capitalism, systemic criminalization has continually marginalized and harmed BIPOC and LGBTQ+ communities in Los Angeles. These oppressive systems perpetuate cycles of violence, disconnection, and disenfranchisement, separating people from their power, health, and potential. The criminal justice system, designed to punish rather than heal, exacerbates these inequalities, leaving communities fragmented and vulnerable.

At TSIC, we build power in criminalized BIPOC and LGBTQ+ communities through stigma-free organizing, mutual aid, and leadership development. Our work is rooted in storytelling, education, cultural expression, intergenerational healing, and intersectional coalition-building. We believe healing comes from within communities when people are given the resources, care, and support to reclaim their lives and futures.

By addressing the root causes of harm—economic inequality, trauma, and lack of access to basic needs—we create spaces for community members to reconnect with their values, health, and power. Our approach centers on restorative justice and transformative justice practices, focusing on care rather than punishment. This means deconstructing harmful systems and rebuilding them with community-led solutions that promote healing, accountability, and empowerment.

TSIC's mission is to empower criminalized BIPOC and LGBTQ+ communities through care-centered, stigma-free initiatives that foster leadership and systemic change. We envision a Los Angeles where every community member, regardless of their past involvement with the justice system, is supported, empowered, and able to create new futures. Our ultimate vision is a society rooted in compassion, care, and intergenerational power, where systems of punishment are replaced with systems of healing.

Systems of criminalization have only deepened harm and fractured lives. True healing begins within individuals and communities, and it flourishes when people are provided the support and tools to see their value and step into leadership roles. Our theory of change is grounded in the belief that when we replace punishment with care and trauma-informed support, we transform harm into healing.

TSIC facilitates this change by providing educational programming, mutual aid, and leadership development centered on storytelling, harm reduction, and restorative justice. Our programs—including expungement services, reentry support, and mental health initiatives—offer people the chance to reclaim their power and disrupt the cycles of criminalization.

One of our most innovative solutions is the use of technology to streamline and humanize expungement services, which are developed by and for justice-involved individuals. We pair lived experience experts with trauma-informed volunteers, creating a leadership pipeline that empowers those directly impacted by the justice system. These leaders then help drive community solutions that prioritize care and get to the roots of harm, breaking the cycle of criminalization.

Our approach not only addresses immediate needs—like clearing records and providing reentry services—but also builds sustainable pathways to long-term healing and empowerment. By centering storytelling and lived experience, we generate new narratives of resilience, creating lasting cycles of healing, justice, and systemic change.

Finding redemption after incarceration is a journey marked by challenges, self-reflection, and profound transformation. Forgiveness remained elusive as I stepped into the uncertain terrain of freedom, a distant shore on the horizon. The weight of societal expectations, compounded by the shadow of past mistakes, threatened to engulf me in a sea of self-doubt and recrimination. But if I could do it, then so can many others.

The journey toward self-forgiveness was fraught with obstacles—it was a labyrinth of self-imposed expectations and societal norms. As an overachiever navigating the complexities of reintegration, I grappled with the lingering stigma of incarceration—the silent specter that haunted both job applications and social interactions alike. Each instance of my past transgressions was a painful reminder of the barriers between me and societal acceptance. But I have forgiven myself—it is what has grounded me the most.

In Los Angeles, where I live, there are nearly one million working-age individuals. Almost 13 percent of the population have felony convictions, with half entering the criminal legal system living at or below the poverty level. Shockingly, there are an estimated 40k collateral consequences, primarily economic sanctions exacerbating post-conviction poverty. Collateral consequences refer to the additional penalties, restrictions, or disadvantages individuals face due to their involvement in the criminal legal system even after completing their sentence or probation. These consequences can extend beyond the direct legal penalties imposed by the court. They can significantly impact various aspects of an individual's life, including employment, housing, education, voting rights, and access to public benefits.

Many individuals do not even realize that they have the right to petition the courts to have their records expunged. As expungement does not have a universal definition, many people are unaware of this opportunity. Traditionally, one must be well-resourced to petition the courts through a private attorney. For poor people, this often means utilizing the very same institutions that were neglectful of their needs in the first place. This can cause additional trauma and force one to lose faith in a process that they have every right to access.

While criminal justice reformers and political figures have fought for several policies to support folks' reintegration into society, it is still an alarmingly slow process. Therefore, my organization, TSIC, decided to do expungement work. It is a burdensome process that needs more investment, more education for the community, and streamlining to make it a faster response to the needs of people who often times suffer greatly due to poverty.

However, the pursuit of redemption within a system marred by systemic racism is fraught with complexity—it is a delicate balancing act between personal introspection and collective action. It requires individuals to confront the uncomfortable truths of their past, acknowledge the harms they have inflicted, and actively work toward dismantling the systems of oppression that perpetuate cycles of violence and harm. It is truly up to us to build and fight for the world we deserve. I invite you to dream of a world that prioritizes people, moves away from punishment and toward redemption with me.

Today I am grateful for life, my wife, and the freedom I enjoy. I remind myself daily that dismantling the system one chain at a time is worth fighting for. May everyone walk not just break one chain but all the chains that oppressed communities have experienced.

Recommended Assignments

Reflective Essay on Abolitionist Praxis

Objective: To encourage students to reflect on how the themes and personal stories in *Harm to Healing* illustrate abolitionist principles, emphasizing the connections between personal narratives and broader systemic issues and challenging conventional views on crime and punishment.

Instructions:

- Write a 3–5-page essay reflecting on how the author's lived experiences connect to abolition principles as described in the book.

- Consider the following questions in your reflection:
    - How do the author's personal experiences with incarceration and reentry challenge conventional narratives about crime and punishment?

    - What are the specific systemic failures highlighted in the book, and how do these relate to the need for abolition?

    - In what ways does the author's storytelling offer a vision for a world beyond prisons and policing?

- Use specific examples and quotes from the book to support your analysis. Focus on the chapters that discuss the impacts of mass incarceration, the failures of the criminal justice system, and the journey toward healing and community resilience.

Community Action Project: Designing a Mutual Aid Toolkit

Objective: To empower students to apply abolitionist principles of mutual aid and collective care described in *Harm to Healing* by creating a practical resource that addresses a community's need without relying on punitive systems.

Instructions:

- Using the concept of mutual aid as described in *Harm to Healing*, design a practical toolkit to address a specific need in a community impacted by criminalization (e.g., access to housing, mental health support, food security, or legal aid).
- The toolkit should include:
  - An overview of the community needs being addressed.
  - A step-by-step guide for organizing a mutual aid effort, such as starting a food distribution network or a support group for formerly incarcerated individuals.
  - Resources for accessing support (e.g., community organizations, legal aid, housing resources).
  - A section on maintaining a trauma-informed approach and ensuring the effort is inclusive and stigma-free.
- Students should present their toolkit in class or submit a digital version to share with local community organizations.

Storytelling Workshop: Sharing Narratives of Resilience and Resistance

Objective: To explore the power of storytelling as a tool for social change, emphasizing abolitionist values by creating narratives that humanize those impacted by systemic injustice and challenge dominant punitive narratives.

Instructions:

- Organize a storytelling workshop where students create and share a personal narrative or a fictional story inspired by the themes of *Harm to Healing*.

- The story should focus on themes such as:
    - Resilience in the face of systemic oppression.

    - Experiences of incarceration and the challenges of reentry.

    - Visions of a community-centered future beyond imprisonment.

- Students can choose their medium (e.g., written story, spoken word, video recording).

- After sharing their stories, discuss how storytelling can be a form of resistance and how it helps to reshape public perceptions of criminalized communities.

Notes

1. Prison institution chronos are official documents used within the California Department of Corrections and Rehabilitation (CDCR) to record significant events, observations, and actions related to an incarcerated individual's behavior, participation in programs, and overall progress during their incarceration

2. Mr. Or C/O Brown was a kind senior officer who was all too familiar to me as he had worked at my junior high school. He had a unique ability to connect with people and meet them where they were at.

Bibliography

Alexander, Michelle. 2010. *The New Jim Crow: Mass Incarceration in the Age of Colorblindness*. New York: New Press.

Davis, Angela. 2003. *Are Prisons Obsolete?* New York: Seven Stories Press.

Gilmore, Ruth Wilson. 2001. *Golden Gulag: Prisons, Surplus, Crisis, and Opposition in Globalizing California*. Berkeley: University of California Press.

Wacquant, Loïc. 2009. *Punishing the Poor: The Neoliberal Government of Social Insecurity*, Durham, NC: Duke University Press.

Index